The Intimate Act of Choreography

The Intimate Act
of Choreography

Lynne Anne Blom and L. Tarin Chaplin

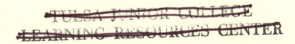

University of Pittsburgh Press

Published by the University of Pittsburgh Press, Pittsburgh Pa. 15260
Copyright © 1982, University of Pittsburgh Press
Feffer and Simons, Inc., London
Manufactured in the United States of America

Library of Congress Cataloging in Publication Data

Blom, Lynne Anne, 1942–
The intimate act of choregraphy.

Includes bibliographical references and index.
1. Choreography. I. Chaplin, L. Tarin. II. Title.
GV1782.5.B55   792.8'2   82-2056
ISBN 0-8229-3463-9   AACR2
ISBN 0-8229-5342-0 (pbk.)

To our parents

Contents

viii / **Contents**

Foreword

An unprecedented interest in dance has swept across the country during the past decade. This development has been visible in the theaters where attendance has grown substantially. The same excitement has been apparent in colleges and universities where dance has become a major focus for many students.

Paralleling this development in dance, there has been a general and growing interest in creativity—its nature and development. Psychologists and others concerned with human development have been persistent in their search for better understanding of the creative process.

Today we find that many teachers of dance are searching for a fuller understanding of the creative process. We know that the choreographic process is dependent on inner sensing, imaginative response, and aesthetic shaping of the inner experience. The question is—how does one assist the young dancer-choreographer in discovering the inner way of experiencing and in allowing the imaginative forming of movement to develop and mature?

In *The Intimate Act of Choreography*, the authors present an approach to the creative process in dance that is comprehensive and philosophically consistent. They base their approach on the assumption that dance as art comes from an inner source. The focus throughout is on the transformation of felt experience into externalized forms.

The suggested experiences range from sensitive improvisations for beginners to complex dance forms for advanced students. They envision a learning environment that facilitates a gradual enrichment and understanding of the craft and form aspects of choreography.

The book is unusual in the way it integrates a consistent concern for process that develops the individual's creative potential with a sequential progression of experiences that contribute to an understanding of dance as a performing art.

Alma M. Hawkins
Professor Emeritus, UCLA

Preface

The rapid growth that dance as an art form has enjoyed in the twentieth century has led to significant development and refinement in the art of choreography. The practice of this art—the actual doing of choreography—has raced far beyond the literature that describes it. Dance critics write articles and books that evaluate the choreographic aspects of dances that have already been created. Dancers have written books on choreography to express their own philosophy. But by far the greatest amount of knowledge and information on choreography exists in the minds and words of choreographers as they teach and create. What we have tried to do in this book is, first, to synthesize the extensive core of knowledge about the process, art, and craft of choreography into a comprehesive reference work; and second, to present a workable format for learning that material, ranging from the fundamental elements of choreography to the more complex issues faced by intermediate and advanced choreographers.

The format we developed evolved from the idea that improvisation is a good way to learn choreography. This approach is very much in harmony with the widely accepted, open-ended modern dance philosophies that value and stress the unique input of each individual's creativity. A highly structured, well-guided improvisation focused on a specific element of dance composition gives the student a physical experience in that particular element. Such experiential learning by doing builds intuitive and kinesthetic knowledge in combination with intellectual understanding.

It is well recognized in current teaching methods that a sense of personal discovery can be crucial to the acceptance of, and belief in, new or unfamiliar ideas. So, whenever possible, the choreographic concept we present is implicit in the improvisational structure. Sometimes it is tucked behind a nonconceptual mask (image), and sometimes the improvisation deals directly with the movement and/or choreographic element being explored. This makes it possible for the student to experience the idea and then, at some level (consciously or not), discover the concept or a tiny hint of it for himself.

Each concept is discussed; improvisations are suggested; then a choreographic study is given to serve as a context for shaping, forming, and reflecting on the concept. In some cases these improvisations and studies are preceded by some initial exploratory work or are followed by discussions. This adds the dimension of personal input, allowing participation before, in the formation of, and after the experience. When only a short movement experience is sufficient to trigger the understanding of a concept, it is provided by an exercise called "Short & to the Point."

The material in the following chapters covers the what and how of choreography. It presents a philosophic approach to choreographing and philosophies about choreographing, but should not be considered a philosophy of choreography; therefore it is compatible with any approach. The information supplements that which a teacher gives in class, or it can serve as an independent source on topics which she doesn't have time to deal with. The material in the book can be adapted to show how she has personally applied the basic elements of the craft and molded them artistically. The teacher may want to read the Teacher's Addendum prior to reading the text; it presents various problems she may face and suggestions for dealing with them successfully.

The Intimate Act of Choreography is designed for a variety

of people within the dance world: teachers who are seeking fresh ideas and valid new approaches to use with young choreographers; serious dance students who are interested in both the practical and theoretical aspects of the art; and dancers who have been teaching for years and are just starting to choreograph, or who have been choreographing and are just beginning to teach their art.

The book can be used as a source book for all levels of choreography and improvisation courses. As suggested reading it can add important dimensions in such courses as Dance Education (theory and philosophy), Teaching Methods, and Children's Creative Movement. Selected sections from the chapters on form, abstraction, style, and tangents can also serve as readings for Dance Aesthetics.

The depth and scope of material covered in our book is comprehensive enough to prepare a dancer for choreographing a full-length dance. Were one to actually work through all the material covered in this book it would take years; the chapter on group work alone, for instance, has enough improvisations, exploratory work, and choreographic assignments to complete a very full semester. The book does not pretend to provide a set of choreographic rules; rather it offers an isolated and comprehensive exploration of each of the many elements that collectively comprise the process of choreography. These are set within a contextual framework of options and choices for the choreographer's, teacher's, and student's consideration.

We acknowledge that artistic genius cannot be taught, but believe that the basic process and tools of the craft can be. No set of concepts will ever take the place of an enthusiastic idea, an inspired motivation, a compulsion to move, dance, and create. Choreography demands inventiveness, judgment, and insight on the part of the student and teacher both. The method in this book seeks to kindle each of these stages and optimize their use by the emerging choreographer.

Lynne Anne Blom

L. Tarin Chaplin

Acknowledgments

The act of teaching implies giving. A devoted educator gener-ously shares with his students the knowledge, materials, and insights he has gained from years of study, experience, and liv-ing. Some of these students in turn become educators and the cycle repeats—essentially making the originally communicated ideas a gift to the public domain and to humanity. The creative educator need not guard his knowledge nor patent it, for he is ever going on to new ideas and integrations on other levels. He will also probably have taught his students to take what he taught not as *the* way, but as *a* way, and encourage them to seek their own ever changing, developing ways. Hearing about the adaptations, progress, and achievements that former students have made with their ideas and material bring such educators continued rewards over the years.

We ourselves owe much to many of our own fine teachers, some of whose ideas have come to blossom in this book: Alma Hawkins, Mary Whitehouse, José Limón, Fé Alf, Marion Scott, John Martin, Carol Scothorn, Louis Horst, Valerie Hunt, Philip Klass, and Norman Lloyd.

In collaborating to write this book, we acted as each other's catalyst, devil's advocate, and censor. Often we coaxed each other's unformed hunches, intuitions into existence. With a shared viewpoint we synthesized mind and material to speak through the single voice of the book.

xvii

As self-critical and challenging as our interaction was, we realized how useful it would be to have feedback from a few people who represented a range of professional expertise. For their insights, care, and encouragement, we thank Eugenia Haney, Joan Griffin, Ruth Wortis, John Morreall, and Peter Ruddick, Carol Walker, Ben Blom, Al Fippinger; and for her editorial meticulousness, Catherine Marshall. They helped us to identify missing or hazy details and to include a variety of points of view; they called us on generalities, glib remarks, or trite explanations.

For their patience, love, and support, Daniel and Aric.

Terminology

Choreographic Study. A choreographic study is an exercise in the craft of choreography. No matter how short, the study should stand by itself; it should have a beginning, middle, and end, and be about something. It should be set clearly (so as to be repeatable) and ready to be shown and discussed.

Discussion. At the end of an improvisation or choreographic study, a discussion often adds to the experience by providing a time to pause, reflect, and evaluate. The discussion can range from sharing subjective feelings about participation in the improvisition ("How did it feel?") to constructive dialogue on how the choreographic study worked in relation to the concept and assignment. In the instances where we have specific comments for discussion, we will present them; in some other cases we will just remind you that a discussion would be advantageous. We have found that once a group is used to sharing their thoughts, experiences, images, and insights, the discussions evolve naturally and are tremendously valuable. For further discussion of this, see the Teacher's Addendum.

Ending. Ending is not just stopping; it is letting the movement find its own conclusion. It entails being sensitive to the natural phrasing and allowing the movement to resolve or come to a close. Don't be rushed by others who may have finished before you; obey your internal timer.

Image.   Imagery is both a way into involvement and a vehicle to take you beyond yourself and your preconception of how an improvisation should be realized. Use it for what it can do for you and then let it go. (This is discussed more fully in the Teacher's Addendum.)

Neutrality.   To begin an improvisation, one must be centered, uncluttered. It's important to leave personal problems at the studio door so one can be clear and receptive, an open vessel, ready to respond. One way to achieve this is by taking thirty seconds or so to reach a neutral beginning. The following type of lead-in can help: "Find your own space [standing, sitting, lying down, etc., as apropos to the improv]. Close your eyes; focus in on your own body-self as you are at this moment. Let go of any extraneous thoughts, becoming neutral. . . ." We will use the symbol ϕ to represent neutrality.

Play.   The improvisations should be approached in a spirit of play. Play implies choices and lack of constraints, yet there is a seriousness to it. A successful improvisation contains the same elements; so follow in any direction that the material takes you for as long as it holds your interest. Remember that play is enjoyed for its own sake, without the necessity to produce; later, you may cull. When we encourage you to "play with it," we mean to "create with it" with an eye toward, but without obligation for, an end product.

Note: Since dancers, choreographers, and teachers come in both sexes, we use the pronouns "he" and "she" interchangeably.

The Intimate Act of Choreography

1 /
Approach

Many people have beautiful, creative ideas for dances, but few of these are ever realized as choreographic entities. One of the main reasons for this is that it is hard to know how to get from the idea, the flash of insight or inspiration, to the fully completed presentation.

You do not learn to choreograph by reading about it, hearing about it, or by watching the major companies in concert. You learn by choreographing, by experimenting, by creating little bits and pieces and fragments of dances and dance phrases, by playing with the materials of the craft over and over again until they become second nature. You learn by getting your ideas out and into movement, onto a body (yours or someone else's), giving your dance an independent existence. But where does one begin? and how? Can choreography be taught? Every book on creativity, after paying respect to the flash of insight, discusses discipline and technique of the craft, and the craft of choreography, like a symphony, includes a wide range of parts.

Isolating Choreographic Elements

In building an understanding of these parts—the concepts fundamental to choreography—it becomes necessary to focus on one at a time. While we separate in order to analyze, we know that any one aspect does not exist independently of another; you cannot deal with time in movement without involving space and energy as well. Yet we will analyze and deal with them separately in theoretical and practical terms for educational ends: to help identify their nature and the extent of their potential. The separation fosters an awareness of their distinctiveness. For example, curved space need not be linked with sustained flow, although almost invariably it will be dealt with in this way, especially by beginners. Some elements seem naturally to call forth or be affined to others as in Laban's Effort/Shape affinities.[1] By providing movement experiences and resulting discussions that isolate the one element in question (such as curved space), and approaching it via many different possibilities of time and force (percussive/sustained, fast/slow, strong/gentle), we help isolate, for example, the concept "curved" and its purely spatial nature. The reintegration of the parts occurs naturally since it is inherent in the phenomenon of dance.

Combining Theory and Practice

Choreography is often taught using the "knowledge by description" method, whereby the teacher gives instructions (which may or may not include discussion of the choreographic concept) and then makes the assignment. An example may be described or even shown. The teacher's input is cognitive, leading to a head approach rather than an organic one. Exploration in working out the problem is limited. There is a tendency to use the initial and therefore standard or most familiar response. How many times have we heard from beginning choreographers, "I spent hours in the studio, but nothing came"; worse yet, what is produced is thin or trite. So while the student may have explored, experienced, and created in completing the assignment, it is possible that the fundamental principles underlying the exercise have not been touched upon. If lucky, the dancer was inspired and the responses creative.

To achieve a synthesis of intuitive and rational knowing, we will be using neither the knowledge-by-description nor the sink-or-swim method. Our approach will be to provide situations, in the form of improvisations, where learning results from experience. This is the way life teaches. One result of this method of teaching is that the student acquires tacit knowledge—knowing something without being able to explain what it is or how you know it, like the taste of a banana; you know it because you have experienced it. Our approach also allows for intuition to come into play ("Intuition," says Emily Dickinson, "picks up the key that memory has dropped"). Learning by experience is strong, and primal; it precedes knowledge by description. All teaching should use both methods, so that explicit knowledge rests on tacit knowledge, and theoretical and practical knowing can augment and enrich one another. Since dance is so primal, it makes even more sense that choreography be taught in this way. The improvisations serve as a preparation, a mental-physical-emotional "seeding of the bed" out of which your choreography will grow. If, as Murray Louis says, "improvisation is the practice of creativity," then choreography as a skill which can be taught and learned is the means and the method whereby creativity can be structured.[2] This approach then is *organic*, which is a major, perhaps *the* major, prerequisite needed to produce solid choreography.

The improvs (*improv* is a commonly used, short form of *improvisation*) are a way of putting the analyzed, theoretical material into the soma-psyche (body-spirit). Metaphorically, the improv is a river whose banks, although they define the overall shape and flow of the waters, are elastic and permeable. They are the instructions or outline of the improv as articulated in this book or by the improv leader; they define the choreographic element to be focused on. The waters are the actual movement responses that flow within and between the banks, the dancers' exploration of the specific focus of the improv.

Using Improvisation

"Dance improvisation fuses creation with execution. The dancer simultaneously originates and performs movement without preplanning. It is thus *creative movement of the moment*."[3] Improvisition is a way of tapping the stream of the subconscious without intellectual censorship, allowing spontaneous and simultaneous exploring, creating, and performing. Improvisation emerges as an inner-directed movement response to an image, an idea, or a sensory stimulus. We do not say you have to improvise in order to choreograph. We accept the idea that movements, like ideas, can spring full-blown and fully formed from the creator. We do say that improvising is one good way to experience and learn choreographic concepts.

Once the choreographic concepts are experienced improvisationally, they begin to become internalized. With time, these experiences will be automatically incorporated into your way of working. There will be no outside set of rules to remember each time you put a dance together, no check list, no do's or don'ts; only a richer store of experience from which to draw, and possibly a few tricks of the trade to lean on in moments of despair.

Learning includes experiencing, analyzing, reflecting, integrating, and evaluating. Analyzing separates and defines, allowing attention to detail and clarity; the process of reflecting adds objectivity and develops perspective; integrating synthesizes, yields understanding, and spurs creativity; evaluating develops a critical eye and discriminating judgment. They are not separate processes but an interwoven one: separate . . . to view objectively . . . to integrate at a different level . . . to redefine again . . . to create anew. The entire process is constantly at work. So we analyze dance into its components, experience them in improvs with an eye to specific detail, critique the results, but in actuality we are already experiencing them as an integrated whole—as dance.

The improvising spirit allows itself to be carried along,

ready to indulge in (and take advantage of) whatever visions present themselves; ready too, to follow the "road less taken." The choreographing spirit sees the fleeting images, the barely noticed motions, imprinting them internally as it continues on its way. Improvising and choreographing become one as the processes (creating movement and critically crafting and forming it) work together. As the movement is flowing out, it is being shaped and developed by intuition interlocked with skill into a finer and finer organic, aesthetic whole.

To all of this, the choreographer brings an inner attitude, a commitment to create, mold, and give form. The intimate act of choreography is an inner process, begun in a creative encounter with movement and pursued and refined with aesthetic sensibility.

2 /
Essentials

Know what your intention is—then say it with clarity and simplicity.

Intention, Motivation, and Clarity

Short & to the Point
Put your arm out. Gather something and bring it in. Try it with different intentions: evil, caring, sneaking, tenderness, teasing, hoarding, loving, destroying, saving.

Let's face it, we should know what we are trying to say with movement. Part of this responsibility lies with the dancer, but it is the choreographer who must not only choose and create the movements, but imbue them with an interpretation, an attitude, a purpose. She is the one who envisions the piece and motivates its growth.

There is no rule that says which comes first—theme, intention, motivation, or even a specific movement phrase. Choreography "is brought into the world in a number of ways: through the senses or the mind; through the heart or the gut; into the fingers or the eye or the backbone or the legs."[1] The trigger varies from time to time and from person to person. Sometimes there is an inner necessity to grapple with, shape, and communicate some pressing idea, creating a passion that forces the blood to speak through the muscle. In dance, such passion can lead to an inspired work if and when the choreo-

8

graphic realization of the idea is fresh and creative in its own unique way.

But this is not always the case. Sometimes there isn't a clear intention; there is only an inner drive, a restless energy, vague and undirected, a need to create. And sometimes for a while that vague nudge has no clearly defined, identifiable intent or theme. Often the choreographic process itself includes discovering and defining the theme and intention. The choreographer goes to the studio and begins to work, and in the working, in the moving, something happens, something connects, something becomes important, and almost on their own, the theme and intention self-clarify.

Alwin Nikolais describes his highly intuitive approach: "I prefer to drop a simple; single idea into my brain and let it rummage around for several months, with no particular efforts toward consciousness on my part. Then, two or three weeks before I begin to choreograph, I attempt to cast up the results of the Rorschach process. Then I like to choreograph swiftly and within a short span of time. I feel that in this outpouring I keep the channels of my subject open. Even here, I do not over-question it."[2]

Paul Taylor says, "I don't know where the ideas come from. If I waited for inspiration, I'd never get anything done. Choreography is a craft after all. I just get busy in the studio and sometimes when I start I haven't got a clue what we're going to do. I just start. If it doesn't lead anywhere, then I start over. But once you get going it doesn't have to be the beginning or the middle or the end of a dance. I find that it takes over if you let it. There's no lack of ideas; it's harder to eliminate them and get what you want."[3]

Such "getting what you want" refers to clarity of intent— and the clearer you are about your intent, the more specific you are, the better chance you have to get your idea across. "With clearness of articulation there comes clearness of communication," says Murray Louis.[3] It is this clarity and intention that is of concern to us as creative and communicative artists. The point that William Strunk makes about written composition applies to dance composition as well: even if you are being intentionally obscure, do so clearly; go roundabout in a straightforward fashion.[5] There is a distinct difference between a dance being chaotic and a dance making a clear statement about chaos.

As the intention and theme become clear and a purpose and plan emerge, motivation continues to provide the energy, endurance, resiliency, and sense of humor that keeps you going. *Motivation* is that inner drive or impulse that causes a person to do something. It can make you do a hundred pliés or improvise on some image for hours, throwing out endless amounts of material because they are not exactly right. It is clarity of intention at an intuitive or rational level which helps you to determine which material fits and which can be thrown away.

"What do you want your audience to take home with them?" asks choreographer Marion Scott, when teaching. That points to everything from "What is your choreographic intention?" to "Why are you doing this piece?" to "What are you trying to say?"

"If I could say it, I wouldn't dance it," comes the reply.

Too often, that is an easy way of avoiding the issue, for the choreographer must know (and know very specifically) what her intention is. It is not enough, for example, to want to present or elicit fear—precisely what kind of fear? Anxiety, fright, apprehension, temerity, paranoia, shyness, terror, dread, shock? Is the dancer threatened, trapped, endangered, timid, alarmed, uneasy, panic-stricken, dismayed, or frantic? The same holds true for movement that is not emotionally motivated: in doing an arm circle are you interested in its gravity and momentum, taking advantage of the suspension at the crest? Do you want the descent controlled? Is the arm weak, flaccid, loose, passive, or limp? If the motion speeds up, how and when is that accomplished? The motion and emotion of the gesture have to be made explicit, as do its cause, focus, purpose, and relationship to the other dancers and the rest of the dance.

Fortunately, we are dancers. We do not have to verbalize all the miniscule aspects of our intention. It's fine if we can or wish to, but as Carol Scothorn says, admonishing her students at UCLA, "Show it. We have to see it. It can't stay in your head."

What *it* is varies. The choreographer's intention can run the gamut from delighting the eye (or confusing it) to spurning insights, arousing memories, eliciting emotional or kinesthetic responses, raising consciousness. It can express the joy of moving, provide surprises, or exasperate.

Anna Sokolow says that in *Rooms* she "wanted to do something about people in a big city. The theme of loneliness and noncommunication evolved as I worked. . . . I have never told stories in dance, though I have always been strongly dramatic. I never plan a dance. I do it, look at it, and then say: 'Yes, I see what I am trying to do,' . . . [as in] 'Dreams,' which was my indictment of Nazi Germany. When I started, I had only the idea of dreams, but they became nightmares, and then I saw they were related to the concentration camps. Once this has happened, I intensified the theme by focusing on it."[6]

Choreographic intention exists on both conscious and preconscious levels. That is why it so often happens that a spectator will see something in a piece that the creator hadn't actually planned on. Possibly it was not the main intention, but part of a hidden or unrecognized one, latent in the labyrinth of the choreographer's subconscious. The spectator's discovery will also be due in part to what he brings to the piece from his own experiences and ideas. Remember that you, as creator, only provide the feast; you cannot control how it will be eaten, what it will taste like on different palates, when it will be digested. What you *can* control is the extent to which you "make the outer in harmony with the inner feelings."[7] Every movement in your dance must serve that dance and that dance only. If you are true to this principle in your choreography, all the movements will be valid and help fulfill your intention.

Theme

Intention makes use of a *theme* as its vehicle. A theme is analogous to the syllabus for a course, the plot or story line of a play; it is that which all else clusters around, your subject; or it can simply be the dance's face, its personality. Usually the more specific it is, the better your chances for clarity. There are millions of themes, though not all of them are suitable for dance. But they do tend to fall into general categories, and it is a good idea (especially for the emerging choreographer) to try a variety of them: a drama or story, personal relationships, the basic elements of movement (space, time, energy) and combinations thereof, pure movement themes, symbolic themes, characterizations, tangibles and intangibles, styles. A given theme could have any of several treatments. For instance you could deal with prejudice symbolically (squares/circles), in terms of characters (slave/master), stylistically (classical ballet/modern dance), motionally (strong, harsh movements/sweet, gentle ones), or dramatically ("Kill the Martians; they're green"). Of course, there are crossovers among these in which one or more are combined in pursuit of your specific intent.

Whatever the theme, the important thing is that it can be expressed in movement. Metaphysical issues, theories of political systems, socioeconomic paradigms—these are simply not suitable dance material. Leave them to the academicians and philosophers, where such analysis and intellectual pursuits rightly belong. This does not, of course, preclude the creation of dances that make social commentary or take stands on moral or political issues. However, all-encompassing themes, such as "all the possible relationships between two men," are unrealistic choreographically because of their tremendous breadth or their too general nature.

Over the years, choreographers have drawn their themes mainly from dance movement itself (all the aspects of the human body moving in time and space molded by a sense of form and style), or from man (his passions and his relationships).[8] According to Merce Cunningham, "the ideas of the dance come both from the movement and are in the movement."[9] José Limón said, "It was Doris Humphrey who first taught me that man is the fittest subject for choreography. And Martha Graham continues triumphantly to prove that his passions, grandeurs, and vices are the ingredients of great dance, great theatre, and great art."[10]

Simplicity

Dealing as we are in the larger-than-life arena that the stage is, tackling the complexities of the human condition, of the boundless possibilities for body movement, of theme and anti-theme, the overriding criterion is simplicity. Simplicity does not preclude complexities, subtleties, and nuances, but it does demand that they be presented in a perceivable and more or less accessible fashion. Accessibility to the viewer depends in turn on the artistic or philosophic goal: should dance be pure entertainment, served up for easy consumption, appreciation, comprehension? or should it be a challenge to the spectators' perceptions and ideas? In either case, each detail of the dance must work toward that indentified goal. To paraphrase William Strunk, Jr.: A dance should have no unnecessary parts; this requires not that the choreographer make all his dances short nor that he avoid all detail, but that every movement tell.[11]

Strive for a lean, elegant statement. Such a clear statement emerges when all component parts are coherently channelled to make one instantly perceived and acknowledged artistic truth. It is from such simplicity that one can build a complexity that has integrity, clarity, and purpose. And it is only as we clarify the specifics that we create universals reflecting our collective experiences. Walter Terry, in discussing Martha Graham's work, states: "When in her dances she is concerned with a specific character, situation or plot, she is actually using it as a starting point or perhaps a frame for the revelation of human behavior . . . in order that 'Frontier' may not be just one frontier, but all frontiers—physical, mental, emotional."[12]

Artistic Impact

Know what your intention is—then say it with clarity, and simplicity. As big an order as that is, and as well as you may appreciate and heed its message, there is more. For it is not enough merely to make dances that abide by this guiding and seemingly obvious principle. Limón says, "The artist's function is perpetually to be the voice and conscience of his time."[13] And Pauline Koner's words expand this same idea: "The person who only mirrors his period is not doing what an artist should do: act as a catalyst in society. If he sees only what is, he is not transcending the immediate. The artist should ask: 'How does one challenge this? How does one make life meaningful?' The artist must comment. . . . The work must have a viewpoint."[14] Yet there are artistic works that are intentionally created sans meaning, sans social commentary. Here the artist-choreographer serves a very different, but nonetheless powerful, function, effecting changes in the perceptual world or in the very meaning and range of art itself. Cunningham does this, and so too, in a different but related way, does Murray Louis, who believes the communicative medium of art can lead an audience to new insights, stimulating their senses and "evoking images and sensations that will serve as a link between the outer physical world and the spiritual realm within."[15] Every artist-choreographer knowingly or unwittingly takes a stand and makes a statement beyond the content of the dance itself. Each work reveals his attitudes toward the state of the art, his viewpoint about the function of art.

As a work of art, the dance is as specific as it is universal; it points from the known to the unknown or deepens that which is already understood. As artist, the choreographer's restlessness and sense of urgency about sentience takes him beyond craft, ideally to create a unique statement that will involve the perceiver in some meaningful way: a moment of perspective, of recognition, or skittishness or serenity.

3 /
Speaking Body

What a glorious, subtle instrument choreographers have to work with. Yes, "a dancer's instrument is her body"—but the choreographer's added concern is, "in how many ways can this body be moved, be shaped, speak, so as to produce the desired effect?"

Body Parts

Of course, the entire body with all its parts is always involved in every exercise, improv, technique, and dance. And body parts cannot be separated any more than we can separate time from the space or energy of a dancing figure. Even when there is only one tiny part of the body moving, the rest of the body serves as background for that part and so is active in a visual and choreographic way. But by focusing on the parts as distinct, their unique capabilities and limitations become more apparent.

When considering body parts, don't forget the hair and the joints. Remember too the face, with its limitless capacity for expression. The face is often neglected in technique classes till it becomes fixed—a blank mirror-stare appendage perched atop a highly expressive instrument. Ironically, dancers are all too aware and critical of those disciplines that approach knowing from the neck up; yet again and again, their concentration in class is solely from the neck down. Obviously, either extreme is destructive to the holistic philosophy of most dance artists. So use this chapter as an opportunity to emphasize the face as the pinnacle, physically and conceptually, of the speaking body—eyes, mouth, jaw, neck, cheeks, all.

Improv: Body Discovery
Take a look at your hand. Suppose you'd never seen one before. Notice the slight hollow on the inside, the lines around the bumps. I wonder what it can do. Can it walk? fly? jamble? Come on, hand, try to ripple, spurt, stiffen, quiver, clench, scratch, hang, pulsate, drum, point. Maybe you should give each part of it a chance to move by itself and show off a bit. It likes that. It's getting all excited! It's hopping all over the place. Hey, it's running away. Let it go; go on, get rid of it. Throw it away. I mean, *really* throw it away. You have lots of other parts. [Apply this same process to the face, spine, feet, hips, head, etc. One by one, throw those parts away after you've explored them.] Well, have you gotten rid of everything? Did you throw away your waist, your back? Now throw your whole self away. Get rid of your body. Who needs it anyway? Is it gone? Is it really all gone? Oops, there's your left shoulder and right knee. Oh well, let them have a dialogue. Why not a face and feet duet? Any other parts not used yet? Add them in, another part and another. Get all your body parts talking to each other at once, babbling away. Everyone's talking: no one is listening. STOP! Now let your whole body speak as one. Make one simple statement and end.

Choreographic Study: Body Parts
Gleaning ideas and even perhaps material from the foregoing improvisation, create a short study using only one part of the body.

Complete dances as well as tidbits have been created from just such an emphasis. Giving such isolated attention to one part of the body is nothing new in the world of dance. Sachs cites many cultures having traditional and highly refined hand dances.[1] In Paul Taylor's *Piece Period* one section is devoted entirely to delicate hand mime performed by three women. Such dances achieve their appeal by isolating, articulating, and focusing on a single part of the body. Isolation is used in dance technique classes all the time to refine and strengthen the body so it can be a more expressive instrument. Choreographers should take maximum advantage of this storehouse of body parts.

Building Trust and Sensitivity

Enjoying improvisation and learning to choreograph often include becoming involved with someone else in movement. This calls for a heightened sensitivity of yourself, your instrument, your partner, and your relationship as you co-create.

Beginning improvisations for two people are extremely simple and for that very reason can be quite difficult; there is no busy work to hide behind. Some of these exercises are used in sensitivity groups because they develop an awareness of what the partner is doing and feeling, and of how the participants respond to each other. Usually very little movement occurs in the first few improvs, and the use of energy, timing, and space is somewhat limited. That's fine, for the main focus of these exercises should be on the validity and honesty of the relationship. That kind of solid, open interaction with another can be threatening and sometimes is side-stepped by the use of arbitrary movement to fill in. Be aware of that and work to keep the movement centered on the improv's stated structure; then the true focus of these improvisations, which is the quality of the interaction between you and your partner, will not be clouded.

The mirroring improv (given later in this chapter) has been around for years, but as presented here, pays special attention to the essence of the relationship between the partners and not just to the external resultant movement. The fact that you are moving *as one* is what is important, not the cleverness of the movement or the fact that one person is following another. This change in the intent of the exercise allows a fluid, interacting relationship. It also allows the movement to have a life of its own.

Some of the exercises presented later in this book are intended to include *fun*. Having fun breaks the ice, gets you going. Being silly is spontaneous, and if you can stay involved and not get superficial, it is possible to play with movement in a brainstorming approach. Judgment is left aside.

So, first and foremost, we're concerned with the relationship of two individuals in which the connecting link is of prime importance. Before asking two people to move together, however, it's important to provide one or more fundamental improvisational structures in which they'll get a feel for that vital connection. The Pair Walk, Back-to-Back Conversation, Mirroring, and Blind Shaping are just a few of the preliminary improvs that can be helpful here.

Exploratory Work: Pair Walk

Everyone picks a partner. The pair walks at a medium pace side by side, in a direct line, across the space, both facing in the same direction. Dancer A has the option of stopping at any instant in the walk, remaining stopped for an indeterminate period of time, and starting forward again. Dancer B's task is to cue in on and match his partner's starts and stops as accurately as possible, without looking at her. Take turns so each person gets a chance to be the initiator.

When you've achieved a fairly good sense of this, try doing the walk with BOTH dancers having the option to stop and start. Let this lead to an increased sense of shared flow. Soon the decision will come mutually; eventually the walking stops and starts itself. Reminders will be necessary to keep the emphasis on getting the message via sensations *other than* the visual, since you will naturally and unconsciously try to look at each other for cues. You can use peripheral vision for sensing your partner.

Improv: Back-to-Back Conversation

In partners. Begin by sitting back-to-back. Sit any way that's comfortable.

φ Close your eyes and take a few quiet moments to become conscious of the feel of your partner's back against yours. Slowly start to explore it. Find out as much as you can about your partner by investigating his back. Is he broader than you or narrower, taller? Is his back strong and resilient? Is it straight, firm, inflexible, or yielding and accommodating? Does it feel warm or cool? Can you tell where the neckline is, or anything about the texture of his skin or the clothing he's wearing? Staying attached at the back, start a "back conversation." Remember to listen as well as to speak. Now let the taller person tell the shorter person something very specific—it could be a story, a secret, an idea, a joke, anything. Try and tell it with your back as explicitly as you can so your partner will know exactly what you're saying. Change and let the shorter person tell what he wants to. Remember to let your back be your voice *and* your ears. When you are both finished telling your message, use your back to give your partner's back a back massage. Relax and enjoy it. Gradually bring it to an end; stay in the stillness of the ending for a moment.

Discuss with your partner any things you'd like to share from your experience. See if you understood his message.

Improv: Mirroring

Take a partner. Sit facing each other in identical positions and close your eyes.

φ Become aware of your body and the position it is in. See yourself from the outside. Visualize your partner in the same position, facing you. Slowly open your eyes and either look past her shoulder or at the floor. She is out of focus but still within your field of vision; you can't identify details but you can see how she moves. Try to synchronize your breathing with your partner's. Don't move, but become aware of what needs to move. Probably your partner needs to move in the same way. Gradually start moving, being sure you move as your partner does. You're responsible for mirroring her movements and she, yours. To a viewer you should be moving as one, doing exactly the same thing at the same time. Soon you will realize that the movement has taken over. You are not sure who is leading or following? Good; the movement is. Let the movement become bigger; go with it. Bring it to an end. Discuss it with your partner. Repeat this improv standing up and let the movement take you into space.

Improv: Mirror Corridor

Form two parallel lines facing a partner. Begin by mirroring your partner. As you work, you have the option of moving in front of or behind other dancers up and down the corridor, while you continue to mirror your partner. You may also expand your movement to include interaction with your neighbors. Any such interaction will, of course, be simultaneously mirrored by your partner with the corresponding person. Cumbersome to say, but not to do! ⏀ Begin . . .

Improv: Blind Shaping

Work in pairs. One person closes his eyes, becoming "blind" while other assumes some shape with his own body. The blind person, using touch, has to explore his partner's shape until he knows what it is and then he gets in that same shape himself. Then he opens his eyes and sees how accurate he has been. Do this several times. Then have the blind one use parts of the body *other than* his hands in order to identify the shape so he can re-create it. Change roles so each has a chance to be the blind person.

Improv: Leading

Work in pairs—one leader, one follower. The leader uses one part of her body (say an elbow) to lead one part of her partner's body (perhaps a hip). The follower tries to stay one to two feet away. The leader not only determines the specific movement of the follower, where it goes in space, but also the timing and dynamics. The leader has the option to switch body parts with a simple verbal cue: "your ear follows my heel." Switch as often as you wish, but try to do it without a break in the movement. The leader should consciously design the ending. After getting the follower where she wants him, she tells him to hold.

Then she choreographs herself into a position in relation to him. Repeat, giving the other person a chance to lead.

The above improvisations are easy, fun to do, and put an emphasis on sensitivity to one's partner. For now, that's what we want to pay attention to rather than the choreographic possibilities they could lead to.

These improvs are quiet and at times produce only a minimal amount of movement, but this is where dance starts—from the inside—with an awareness of body and sensitivity to movement, your own and that of the others you'll be dancing with. You should carry that awareness with you, sure as a heartbeat, a primary and integral part of your approach.

4 /
Phrase

Basic Structure

A phrase is the smallest and simplest unit of form. It is a short but complete unit in that it has a beginning, middle, and end. Every phrase, even the shortest, contains this basic structure; it starts, goes somewhere or does something, and comes to a resolution. A phrase is to a dance as a sentence is to a book. Just as a sentence is comprised of separate words, so a phrase is made up of individual movements. But a phrase is not a simple accumulation of movements strung together any more than a sentence is a list of words. Both phrases in language and phrases in dance must make sense. The movements share some common element of intent. So a phrase has form and content. It is a grouping of related movements that have kinesthetic logic *and* intuition, and are connected by their cooperative creation of a unit.

In a dance, phrases are grouped together into larger phrases, then built into longer sequences, and formed into sections. Often a particularly striking one is used repeatedly, like a verse in poetry, or as a motif for development. It is within this context that phrasing functions in building dances.

To discover the importance of the phrase, the following exercise asks you to move *without* a sense of phrasing (one effective method of learning is by contrast). Unphrased movement is not difficult to do, but it is dull to watch for any length of time. That's because phrasing occurs naturally in life as it also must in art.

Short & to the Point: Perpetual Motion
♀ Lie on the floor. Try to roll without any perceptible beginning or end, without any sense of fall and recovery. (Either you will have to go quite slowly, with control, or very fast, possibly beginning and ending offstage.) Do a figure eight with your arm, again with a sense of foreverness, no beginning, no end. Now, find your own perpetual motion movement.

High Point

Learning about a phrase is made easier when the idea of a high point is introduced right along with it, because a high point immediately produces a very noticeable form and is so often a natural part of a phrase. Defining high point is rather sophomoric, for it is such a common occurrence—the peak of a tossed ball, the blowing and bursting of a bubble. Conceptually, for use in dance, we can say it is the most important part of the phrase: the high point may be stronger or faster; it may be marked by an extreme change or by a gradual dynamic build; it may be the sudden cessation of movement; but in any case, it is in some way more arresting to the perceiver. Not all phrases have obvious high points. A unit of movement having no noticeable high point can still be considered a phrase if it has a beginning, middle, and end. In the overall picture, phrases without distinctive high points have their place, as much as potatoes in the stew. We'd be worn out if we were continuously bombarded with an unending series of high points. It would render the true zenith of the dance anticlimactic.

A single movement idea is realized (starts, goes somewhere, ends); the result is a phrase. Two of the most basic ways of creating a phrase are through the use of a movement impulse (an energy surge instigating a full-blown movement) and through breath. The impulse serves as an impetus out of which the movement flows necessarily and organically.

Improv: Impulse—Tilt

ᶲ Begin standing straight. Tilt your body forward in one piece bending only at the ankles. To the side, back. Go as far as you can, keeping your feet anchored. Try tilting in another direction. Another. Now tilt so far that you start to fall and have to step in order to catch yourself. Allow the impetus to propel you in space. Try to go further off-center each time before you start to fall and stop yourself. Get daring with it until you really experience the sense of *it* falling *you*, and you *have* to catch yourself in order to break the fall. Now try running out the momentum produced by the fall—you'll run only as much as the impetus of the fall propels you. Repeat, but this time once the tilt has been initiated, let your body be rubbery.

In this improv the instant when *tilt* becomes *fall* is the high point. It provides a good example of how one action can trigger another; force begets force. Often this is the verve upon which a dance (or dancer) feeds.

Breath naturally and familiarly creates a phrase. It provides another approach to building phrases.

Improv: Breath

ᶲ Standing. Gradually deepen your breathing. Take a long, deep inhalation and slowly exhale. Sense the beginning, middle, and end of each breath, each breath as a mini-phrase. Become aware of the body's natural movement during the inhale (a rising or expanding) and the exhale (a falling or collapse). Let your arm fill with the air of your inhalation and deflate as you breathe out. Pick another body part; how does it breathe deeply? Let the deep breathing continue to be reflected in the movement as you resume normal breathing (so you won't hyperventilate). Try other body parts—torso, head, shoulders, toes. Gradually involve the whole body. Now start panting, like a puppy dog. Let the panting be in your hands, hips, knees. Get it into the whole body. Explore the kind of movement it results in. How does your elbow pant? Let it be in your fingers, your stomach. Once you get it into a part of the body, let your breath return to normal (don't hyperventilate). Put it in your feet and let it take you across the room. Now inhale deeply, taking in as much air as possible; then, all at once, blow it out, *all* of it, with a forceful expiration, "HAH!" Do it again. Strong. Experiment with the kind of movement this produces, in isolated body parts and in the whole body. Slow and full inhale, sudden exhale. Once you have a sense of the type of movement it produces, continue playing with it while returning to normal breathing. Let it move you through space. Randomly mix the three types of breathing and resultant movements.

Discussion. Which of the three types of breathing contains a natural sense of phrasing? Of impulse? Of high point? Which don't? Why?

Deep breathing has a strong sense of beginning, middle, end. We're more aware of its shape as a unit (phrase) than of the high point it contains. One could perhaps distinguish a high point, if picayune, but it is so uneventfully arrived at and left, so subtle, that it may be more useful to look at each deep inhale and exhale more as a well-shaped phrase than as having a true high point. The impulse is quietly, if at all, discernible. *Panting* is a good example of the rather undramatic (i.e., unmarked) type of phrase; there are no particular high or low points. Yet, when executed with changes in body parts or directions, it takes on a shape; it starts, goes somewhere, and stops, and so conforms to the definition of a phrase as having a beginning, middle, and end. *Inhalation with sudden exhalation* gives us two choices, producing a good sense of phrasing in either case. We can consider it as a unit with a gradual beginning, culminating in an exclamation point at the instant of the expiration. Or we could think of the expiration as the beginning, in which case the climax occurs at the inception of the phrase, trailing off from there. In this second instance the strong and forceful exhale serves both as the impulse (the initiator producing a phrase of movement) and as the high point of that movement phrase.

Choreographic Study: Breath
Create a study based on breath. Include all three types of breathing, using the breath audibly throughout. All movements should be breath instigated. Perform twice, with and without the audible breathing.

The overall shape of a phrase is determined by where the high and low points occur. The high point in a short phrase may be at the beginning, at the end, both, or in the middle. (See the diagrams for the next improv.) You can start with a bang, build to a bang (as with a sneeze and the long, agonizing tickle when it's coming, *it's coming*, IT'S COMING . . . !), or build to a bang and die out. These first three are the well-known models diagramed by Doris Humphrey.[1] In the fourth possibility, actually a combination of the first two, the movement created by the initial high point does not die out completely, but regains strength or momentum, carrying on to a second high point at the end.

Remember that these shapes are consciously simplistic, for they apply to shorter aspects of phrasing. Later in the book, when we discuss form, we'll deal with the notion of *climax* as it applies to an entire dance.

The following improvisation may appear rather lengthy, but taking the time to go through each of the four models will be time well spent. Each approach may be seen as a paradigm; each will be used over and over as you progress in your choreographic growth. The exercise is structured so as to provide an experience of high point through all three elements of space, time, and energy via various inputs, including conceptual, dramatic, and qualitative.

Improv: High Point

Remember that each section (a,b, or c) represents a simple phrase, not a long, involved sequence. Keep it short—about ten seconds for each one.

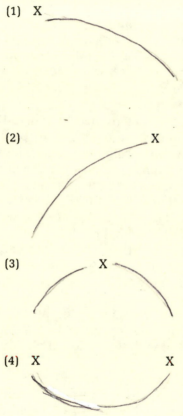

(1) X

a. begin very fast, and gradually die out to as slow as possible
b. begin very big, then gradually become very small
c. begin very strong, and gradually become ever so gentle

(2)

a. starting with continuous flow, become sudden in your movements
b. starting indirect (vague, scattered), focus in and become very direct
c. starting light, become very heavy

(3)

a. stalk your prey, catch him, drag him home
b. processional, the crowning, recessional
c. an elf, turning into a giant who gets shattered to bits

(4) X

a. sparkle . . . droop . . . jiggle
b. hurried . . . lazy . . . excited
c. rubber band . . . feather . . . bullet

Choreographic Study: High Point

Pick two of the four phrase shapes and compose a movement phrase for each one. Try to make them a little longer than what you just did in the improv. Let one of these be based on either a breath or an impulse motivation.

Variety in Phrase Length

There should be variety in the length of the phrases as well as in their shapes. Were any of the phrases in the previous improvs longer or shorter than others? That's understandable, since the length of a phrase is determined by its content; it is as long as it needs to be. Often there is a tendency to make all phrases have the same length—medium. That can become monotonous unless you intentionally want to create tick-tock predictable regularity. It adds both interest and complexity to the dance when the phrases vary in length.

Choreographic Study: Mixing Phrases

Using the Impulse improvisation (p. 25), loosely set three phrases (all of the same length) and put them together. Then make one of the three phrases as long and as extended as possible, while still coming out of the single impulse. Take another of the three phrases and make it as short and concise as possible. Put these two together with the remaining medium-length phrase. Show both the equal-length version and the varied-length version. Which is more interesting? Why?

Choreographic Phrase vs. Movement Combinations

Choreographic phrase is often confused with movement combinations. Most dancers have taken technique classes before beginning to choreograph and often assume that the short movement combinations that they've been learning (as in across-the-floor sequences) are the same as choreographic phrases.

Movement combinations can be merely movements strung together like beads, without notice of their individual shape, color, texture, or relationship to one another. Like letters from a Scrabble set, they can be spilled end-to-end without rhyme or reason, spelling no words, having no aesthetic validity. This may work for drilling technique, but it is not choreography. The purpose of a movement combination is to provide a technical challenge such as coordination skills, strength development, endurance, or spatial discrimination.

A choreographic phrase, however, has a different intention—to convey feelings, images, ideas, to present visual impressions, a story, symbol, or design element. Regardless of what intention it may have, a choreographic phrase has a personality, an identifiable movement "face." The phrase has an "ishness" (as Carol Scothorn would say). It is *about* something. With or without actual meaning, it is expressive; it has flesh, whereas a movement combination often has only bones. A choreographic phrase seeks *to touch the viewer*, to communicate a sense, vision, idea, style, texture, or quality. It has an attitude about it, an aura of uniqueness, a selfhood.

Ideally, movement combinations can and should be choreographic phrases, well formed, aesthetic, and technically challenging. However, when first asked to do choreographic studies, students sometimes (rather innocently) produce "techniquey" movement combinations instead. It is important to clear up this discrepancy in the early stages of a choreographer's education.

5 /
Space

A body exists in space . . . moves in space . . . is contained by space. A dancer's place and design in space, the direction and level she moves in, and her attitude toward the space, all help define the image she is creating. Her focus and the way she shapes space are integral parts of the space. Space is the 3-D canvas within which the dancer creates a dynamic image. Breaking it down into component parts brings a wealth of possibilities for movement exploration.

Space can be considered as an active participant, an abstract partner. What beginning dance student hasn't played with the space that is closing in on her? Yes, movement can make an empty, dead space into a dynamically pulsating one. Mary Wigman repeatedly used space as an active element, sometimes as an opponent. She went even further, actually defining dance as motivated tension in space *and* as a creator of space. Murray Louis introduces space in his *Dance as an Art Form* film series by saying, "In its basic form, space is a void—silent, sterile, innocent—before consciousness, before life." A choreographer must fill and mold that void.

People vary not only in how they see space, but in their spatial affinities; they are more comfortable with, and therefore have a tendency to move in, certain relationships to space. The early German modern dance divided dancers into groups according to this spatial affinity. As classified by La-

31

ban, there were low, middle, and high dancers, the categories being differentiated by level.[1]

Level

Low is about earthiness, being into the ground, having a strong feeling for gravity. The movements range from the heaviness of dragging to the abandon of a wild but earthy folk dance. The main emphasis of middle level is that it facilitates "goingness" and a standing that is on the ground rather than of or into it. And while being the transition between low and high it contains some relation to each. High level is about elevation, flying, and defying gravity. It is also about effortlessness; the dancer is poised above the earth barely touching it, seeming not to need or use the ground. It is epitomized by the illusion the ballet creates, though as every good dancer knows, the secret of that illusion is using the ground.

Levels range from a grounded and rooted low (lying) and a variety of lows (crawling, sitting, kneeling, crouching); through the range of middle (demi plié, standing, relevé and traveling); to high level, which includes elevation (jumps, leaps); and finally the unnaturally, unusually, and artificially high. This last category needs partners, platforms, wings, cables, gimmicks of all kinds, and optical illusions with film and TV (where the dancer is actually lying on the floor but appears airborne).

Improv: Levels

◊ Lie on the floor. Feel everything draining out of you and into the earth below. Grow roots down into the earth. Become a part of the earth. How could you move and still be part of the earth, as on the bottom of the ocean, or a being in the mud? Grow out of the earth just a little. Move on the earth now; let your roots dissolve, break them, or pull them out. Try moving toward your feet, head, side, while still on your belly, on your back or side; try moving in all directions. Drag. Wriggle. Slither. Roll as many different ways as you can. Gradually work yourself up to sitting.

Explore the process of arriving at sitting, as if for the first time. What can you do now that you could not do before? How many ways can you sit? Be a model for an art class, giving them a series of two-second sitting poses. Be a moving piece of sculpture on that level. Can you roll in a sitting position? Try a variety of ways of getting to your knees; try traveling. Crawl on your knees and elbows, knees and hands, feet and elbows. Feel clumsy? . . . use it! Feet and hands. Try it heavy and dragging, or light and "puppylike." Staying on all fours . . .

. . . now take weight off your hands. Gradually come to standing. You are standing but your focus and interest are still down. Feeling heavy, your weight into the ground. Your knees are bent, then gradually straighten. Explore the feeling of being vertical, upright. What is standing all about? Become aware of an ever increasing circle of space around you . . . see the horizon . . . GO! in all directions. Walk . . . go ahead, skip . . . run . . . race. Become aware of the space above you . . . focus up. Reach up into the space. Explore the space above you, grab at it. Try to get there. . . .

Try to fly, sporadically, but still feel earthbound. Let it get bouncy so that you are comfortably part of the space above the ground, even if the space is just an inch above it. Enjoy it. Let it develop into real elevation, high jumps. Defy gravity, leap, FLY! Help someone else jump; lift them up. Use someone or something to help you get higher than ever. Climb on a box, chair. Hang from the barre. Be above the ground. Move as that allows: swing, climb, balance. How does it feel? Is it scary? Use it. Sense the height, the freedom.

Choreographic Study: Levels

Create a study, starting either low or high. Explore that level and then progress through middle to the opposite level. Have some intention line to carry you through, dramatic or not.

Geometry of Space

There are many systems for analyzing space. One can divide it into point, line, direction, dimension, plane, and volume. Of these, direction implies the greatest degree of mobility.

Direction

There are certain images that are best realized in specific directions. Retreat takes us back, while a chase goes forward. We jump up and fall down. Sneaking or shifty movement often goes sideways or on a diagonal. People in a position of authority, who are assertive, aggressive, all move forward.

Improv: Directional Patchwork

As you work on these directions try to include a number of different levels.

♦ Become aware of the front of your body, aware of the space in front of you. Explore it. Take your front into that space. Move ahead with authority. Be assertive, aggressive. Charge. Race! Finish the race in a position of racing. Now, move in a solemn procession, as king, candle-bearer, or slave. Try greeting someone, perhaps a series of positions of greeting.

♦ Your back has eyes; see with it. Explore the space behind you; go into that space. Now instead of emphasizing going into that space, emphasize going away from the space in front of you. Retreat . . . in fear . . . falling, running backward . . . a series of positions of retreating.

♦ Be on the double yellow line between two streams of heavy traffic that whizzes by in front and in back of you. Move along sideways, trying to get to the traffic light at the end of the block. What kinds of locomotion can you use to get there? While staying sandwich-skinny, can you slide, jump, leap, run?

Choreographic Study: Directionality

Create a short study using two or three directions. Possibly work with a dramatic theme (e.g., charge ahead, meet defeat and retreat, and then try to sneak out sideways). Or compose a study based on a full exploration of one direction, on all levels. Keep in mind the possibility of moving diagonally while keeping your body facing the front.

Dimension

Space is also dealt with in terms of the three dimensions: height ($\updownarrow$), width ($\leftrightarrow$), and depth ($\nearrow$). It is possible to zero in on any one of these in movement, making it the primary intent (although, in fact, the movement exists in the dancer's body in three-dimensional form). In moving forward and backward, we explored depth, while sidedness allowed us to investigate width. Up-down (height), being more stationary, wasn't dealt with then. To explore it now we can use the following improv.

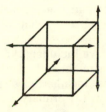

Improv: Dimensionality—Height
Become aware of the space below you. Dig your way down. Sink. Fall. Collapse. As you progress down, go through a number of positions that have the essence of downwardness. Stay down and become aware of the space up above. Desire to be up. Expand up. Reach up. Explore up. Find ways of moving up, higher. Try this a number of times in different ways, alternating between going down and going up.

Plane

Planes are the result of joining any two of the three dimensions and include the vertical, horizontal, and sagittal, which Laban labeled door, table, and wheel.[2]

Plane	A joining of	Referred to by Laban as
the vertical	height and width	the door plane
the horizontal	width and depth	the table plane
the sagittal	depth and height	the wheel plane

In our earlier work with direction, we explored the wheel (or sagittal plane) with the directions of forward and backward. Our work in sidedness can be amplified in terms of the door or vertical plane. For this, it's instructive to look to the ancient Egyptians who were masters of two-dimensional design.

Improv: Egyptian Frieze

One person makes a shape, with emphasis on its two-dimensional design, that is, in the vertical plane. Someone else looks at that shape and takes some accommodating shape along its planar line, as in an Egyptian frieze. People continue to add on, one at a time, creating a wall-like mural of bodies. Before each person adds on his body, he carefully considers the overall design created thus far and tries to make his addition in harmony with it or in response to what he perceives as a need in the total shape.

Variations on the above include: (1) a design that is all flowing-and-curved or all straight-and-angular; (2) spatial discrepancies, either very close together, or spaced widely apart, or a combination of the two; (3) primary attention to variations in levels.

The farther one goes from the centeredness of vertical, the more a sense of tension is created. "Movement in the vertical plane is sensed as stable . . . even when fast movement, such as a spirited jump, propels the body directly upward. . . . However, as the body shift[s] from the vertical [diagonally toward the horizontal] a feeling of imbalance and insecurity [results]."[3] Once a movement reaches the table (the horizontal) plane, it returns to connotations of stability, although of a less active nature than that associated with verticality.

Short & to the Point

You are put between two coverslips of glass and placed under a microscope. Periodically they pulsate, pressing you together and squishing you into all kinds of shapes. Try it on your stomach as well as on your back.

Improv: Table Top

Stand on one leg with the rest of your body parallel to the floor like a one-legged table. Imagine the floor and ceiling as facing mirrors. Staying flat, play with your reflections. Find ways of moving your table across the room. You may change legs as needed.

Cumulatively the directions, dimensions, and planes result in volume, the three-dimensional space that the body actually occupies. We can take that body and compact it (roll it into a tight ball) or expand it (spread it out as big as possible), but in reality the volume of the body remains constant.

Design in Space: Shape

Design can be thought of as a capturing of form. It can be static, as in a pose, tableau, or position that is breathlessly on the verge of arrival or departure. But it can equally be perceived as dynamic, having the cumulative effect of a tracing of motion; for movement moves and disappears by the time we can register it, to be captured in the memory only as a stillness of sorts, a movement picture.

Design—the shape of one or more bodies in space—can be defined according to the lines of the shape (curved or straight-and-angular), the overall shape (symmetrical or asymmetrical), the relation of the shape to space (positive or negative). The viewing of art works, and of sculpture and architecture in particular, are tremendously useful in enhancing one's perception and appreciation of these concepts.

The Lines of the Shape: Curved or Straight-and-Angular[1]

Particularly when executed with purity, curved design and straight-and-angular design show a marked and distinctive contrast in their dramatic implications. Curved and circular lines, still or moving, produce a sense of flow and ongoingness and are affined with sustained timing. They are graceful and lyrical, emphasizing a feeling of resiliency, of suppleness; they are soft, reflecting an attitude of caring and accommodation; they are soothing (a rocking chair, as opposed to a straight-backed side chair), yielding, bending, animallike, organic.

Straight lines and angles give a feeling of stasis, stillness; when done in movement, the movement appears broken or shattered (like a dropped mirror) and cuts through the space; there is an affinity with percussive timing. Concentrated strong and angular movements tend to produce rote and machinelike qualities, automata; they have a sense of directionality; they call to mind strong adjectives and their corresponding themes and ideas: hard-edged, sharp, jagged, rigid. They are unyielding, inflexible, solid.

Exploratory Work
Find and bring in cartoons showing curved and straight-and angular design.

Improv: Curved or Straight-and-Angular
◊ Become aware of the flexibility and suppleness of your body; be soft, relaxed. You are under water and the currents are playing gently with your body; let your body flow like seaweed. Keeping these images, make circles, curves . . . little ones with your hands, big ones with your body. Make ripples. Let your body be swept along, carried easily around many things. Travel on curved paths through space, keeping the curves in your body, curving lines and rounded movements. Find a way to finish that shows, in its stillness, the essence of this way of moving.

Now you are made of wood, a stick figure. Move your parts with clean, clear-cut movements. You are all lines and angles, crooked, every joint a hinge—perhaps like a robot. Be efficient, direct. How does it feel? Stiff? Jerky? Show how it feels. Now move through space in straight, direct paths. You may change directions along corners or angles only—change abruptly, sharply. Find a way to finish that shows, in the end design, the feeling of these actions. Discuss the differences that were noted between the curved and the straight-and-angular movement. Try to identify emotional overtones or suggestive themes and images that each brought to mind.

The Overall Shape: Symmetrical or Asymmetrical

These two ways of analyzing the overall shape have been used repeatedly because of their strong connotations and because they are easily recognizable visually.

Symmetry, in which the design is exactly the same on both sides of center (as in a Rorschach ink blot), produces a feeling of stasis, of strength and authority. Because it is stable and balanced, it indicates surety, control, power. It is the position for weightlifters, policemen, kings. It is the structure that dominates the Capitol, the Eiffel Tower, and the Empire State Building. It is reflected in the Sphinx and in religious symbols.

Asymmetry, on the other hand, inherently possesses and produces tension and a dynamic quality. Even in stillness, an asymmetrical design has a pull and thrust or weightedness in some direction. Because of this, it implies movement, it projects excitement, and when taken to an extreme, even danger. When someone is tipsy, he is off-center, unpredictable, shaky. Asymmetrical movement can be funny or scary or tortuous. It is laden with variety, contrast, complexity. It is risky, whereas symmetry is safe. Asymmetry is the shape of racing, of animals on the hunt. It is the language of distortion, pain, and the grotesque or deformed. It is the Leaning Tower of Pisa, the Grand Canyon, lightning, a car accident, slipping on a banana peel.

Because dance is about moving, about dynamism, its moments of excitement and highest interest are usually asymmetrical, with symmetry being used for contrast and for points of departure or closure. The choreographer must understand the effects of these differing shapes so he can employ them consciously to produce the desired result. Perhaps, for instance, it was because of the emphasis in her technique on fall-and-recovery (and therefore of the balance/off-balance aspects of movement) that the Symmetrical-Asymmetrical contrast was so basic in the choreography of Doris Humphrey.

To make the point, we will define asymmetry as "very unsymmetrical," a position or movement that is not just slightly different on both sides, but decidedly so.

Exploratory Work

Bring in examples of symmetry/asymmetry. Include three-dimensional objects as well, so they can be analyzed in all three dimensions. This is particularly useful since the dancer's body is three-dimensional, and its visual configuration varies according to the position of the viewer—front, back, side, top, bottom, diagonal.

In discussing any design element, but most specifically with symmetry and asymmetry, you need to be aware of how the dancer is facing in relation to the audience. What is symmetrical frontally will always be asymmetrical when viewed from the side (in fact, the human body is always asymmetrical from the side). Of course, when we put two similar bodies in identical positions front-to-front or back-to-back and view them as a unit from the side, they create a symmetrical design.

Improv: Computer

ϙ You are the image on a computer teaching machine. You are programmed for symmetrical and asymmetrical positions incorporating changes of level and use of body parts. As the buttons are pushed [indicated by a verbal cue of "sym" or "asym" by the leader] perform a variety of sym/asym positions.

Improv: Man-on-a-Stick

ϙ You are a toy man on a stick. As the string is pulled by the child, you move. You are built so that you can only move *symmetrically*. Unlike the actual toy, you can move in three dimensions. Move in place—standing, sitting, lying down on your back, front. You have many joints; using them will help you find greater variety. Remember you can work in the three dimensions. At midnight you are allowed one greater freedom—moving through space—but it still must be symmetrical. It's hard. What are the ways you can travel with both sides doing exactly the same thing at the same time? Walking won't work, will it? One side of you has to match exactly what the other side is doing at every instant.

Discuss both improvs. What things were you most aware of when doing symmetrical positions? Asymmetrical? In the Man-on-a-Stick improv, did you have problems getting down to the floor and back up again while maintaining strict symmetry? Why? What does this tell you about falling and rising? Did you feel more constrained doing symmetrical or asymmetrical movement? What are some of the factors that contribute to that? What emotions, overtones, did you experience with the one versus the other? What modes of traveling across space are possible when you are limited to symmetrical movement? Is a walk symmetrical? Why or why not? What's the difference between symmetry in space and symmetry in time? Regularity and repetition add to the sense of symmetry as perceived over time. Glissade assemblé executed to the right and repeated to the left would be considered symmetrical, for it balances (in time) what is happening on the right with what is happening on the left.

Choreographic Study: Symmetry/Asymmetry
Create a study using symmetry and asymmetry. At some point combine the nonaffinities (e.g., move in symmetry and hold positions in asymmetry, or have tensions in symmetry and calm authority in asymmetry).

The Relation of the Shape to Space: Positive/Negative

The relation of the shape to space, and of the space to shape, is a matter of the viewer's perception. It does not exist as an independently identifiable design element in the same way curved or straight-and-angular and symmetry/asymmetry do. The best visual example of positive/negative space is the optical illusion of the vase/face profile drawing (fig. 1). It allows the viewer the choice of perceiving either the black or the white as the object and making the opposite color the surrounding or intervening space. Foreground and background become interchangeable.

Positive shape may be thought of as tangible, as object, as occupying a given amount of space. Negative space is the area between objects, between the positive shapes. By changing or rearranging positive shapes, the intervening negative space is

Figure 1

simultaneously altered. Both have shapes that are malleable, with any change in one resulting in a specific and accommodating change in the other.

A caution is needed here. Don't be misled by the value-laden words *positive* and *negative*. They merely label two different ways of looking at space. In the aesthetics of the Western world, the focus is primarily on positive space, while the Eastern mind is more concerned with the concept of negative space. This is clearly seen in the design of formal Japanese rock gardens, where the aesthetic decisions regarding placement of the rocks are made with attention to the visual and bodily paths one will travel in going from one rock formation to another. The negative space is viewed as the connecting link, the binding force between two points, with the points given less importance than the connection.

Exploratory Work
From a book of M. C. Escher's prints, select those which best illustrate the use of positive/negative space.

Improv: The Air as Clay
Divide the group into watchers and movers. The watchers should first pay attention to the designs of the body, the posi-

tive shapes being made, and then focus on the negative space created by, around, and in between the positive shapes. ◊ Suppose the air was clay and you could be a container. Try making a circle with your arms . . . now squeeze out the clay. Use your body to make another container, such as a hole with your hands. Change its shape. Become aware of your entire body and all the soft clay-air surrounding it and between its parts. By moving your body, mold the clay. Consciously, by what you are doing and how you are moving, alter what's around your body. Attend to the designs that this produces.

Discuss how you could get the audience to attend to the negative rather than the positive shapes.

Focus

If we think of the body as the "temple of a million eyes" we can begin to get an idea of the extent of focusing power a dancer can achieve. Do we want the dancer to relate in a diffused or direct way to the stage space, other dancers, the audience? Do we want the dancer to make a part of his body or a particular spot on stage the focal point of movement or dramatic attention? Do we want the audience to feel that the dancer is encroaching on, escaping to, confiding in, or shrinking from them or something or someone (real or imagined)? The choreographer should consider each of these questions in determining the focus of every movement or phrase. Focus becomes an especially important consideration in dramatic works.

The face itself is a crucial part of focus. It can emphasize the movement's intent with a snarl or sneer (e.g., when Iago in *The Moor's Pavanne* shows the handkerchief to Othello) or it can make a contradictory statement, as in comedy (dancing gaily along with a look of agony).

The term *facing* refers to the orientation of the body in relation to the movement and involves other factors besides the face. Sometimes the intent of the movement includes the necessity for simultaneous, multiple facings.

Short & to the Point
Travel on a diagonal to upstage right, looking over your shoulder at downstage left with your body facing downstage right, doing a movement (with an arm or leg) to upstage left. No problem, right? Now try doing it again, but this time keep as strong a focus as possible to all the facings simultaneously. Make the up-right, down-left, down-right, up-left foci all equally important—both in terms of clarity and in strength of execution.

We can see another aspect of facing by asking the question, "Is this movement or design most effective when seen from the front, the side, or when placed on the diagonal?"

Short & to the Point
Design a simple movement. Perform it facing front, side, back, diagonal. Which is better? Repeat for a movement with multiple facings.

A dancer needs to go far beyond the mere execution of movements; she must emphasize and draw the audience's attention to them. This she does with her entire body. Say, for example, a particular gesture of the hand is to be of primary importance; not just the face, but the chest, thighs, kneecap, shoulder must all have a sensitivity to that hand. They must attend as with eyes of their own.

Carmelita Maracci, master teacher, presented a développé into arabesque this way: "Don't just stick your foot back there! Imagine your leg to be as in a Dali painting, with a large eye at the end of it. Let that eye *find* its way towards the arabesque. Let the pointed foot *seek* its path and pursue it."

Another way in which a secondary part of the body can help focus attention on the primary part is by being less distinctive itself. It becomes neutral so as to have less impact. It exists as background. Conversely, it could actively and overtly lavish attention on the gesture of importance (by actual pointing, looking, or through conscious sensitization).

In either case, these secondary body parts become subservient, sublimated to the main attraction of the moment. Both a clear knowledge of the movement's intention and of how to achieve heightened attention for a specific movement are necessary parts of the craft to be mastered.

Improv: Featured Attraction

♀ Let your attention go to a particular part of your body. Let that part begin to move. It is the soloist; let it do a dance of its own. Make sure everyone is looking only at it. Gradually, the rest of the body starts moving as the chorus, so to speak, for this featured dancer. In what different ways can the body serve as background, still or quiet or with motion of its own. Take your soloist body part through space, across the studio. Try different ways of traveling while continuing to keep attention on that one part of the body. Now shift to another part of the body as "featured attraction" and experiment with it in similar ways ... with stillness, with motion, with locomotion in the rest of the body. Eventually begin to shift back and forth between those two soloists (body parts), focusing now on one, now on the other. Are they having a duet? A fight? An encounter? Are they similiar in their quality of movement, or quite different? Perhaps one is light and smooth, while the other is jerky and percussive. Decide for yourself.

Choreographic Study: Duet of Body Parts

Create a study based on the preceding improv with two primary body parts. You may choose to establish an alternating sequence between them, or the dance may be a progression, a gradual shifting from emphasis on one part of the body to emphasis on another.

Active Space

When the space itself becomes alive, when it has meaning or takes on symbolic suggestions of its own, it is active. In these instances, the space carries import. The choreographic intention, and the dancer's interpretation of that intention, creates life out of otherwise dead space.

Space as Dynamic

Space can be imagined and used as a definite dynamic entity and thereby given a sense of tangible presence. It can be invested with a power of its own (a magnetic force, pulling or repelling). Mary Wigman is probably the choreographer best known for using space as an active opponent.

Improv: Space Creature

A space creature with great magnets on his many appendages is playing with a human toy: you. At first, he is very subtle and gentle, eager to find out how he can make the human being move. The human's attitude is up to you; it may vary. After a while, the creature gets slap-happy. He teases the human by abruptly varying the strength of his magnets and where he places them to pull the human around. ◊ Begin . . .

Space as Symbolic

Symbolic space has a power of suggestion that adds overtones and lends impact to the idea of the dance. It can be created with movement or with sets or special effects. Anna Sokolow in *Rooms* used chairs representationally (symbolically), as home base or enclosures. A circle of light could serve as a safety zone or the womb. The dancers' movements and positions can create spaces, places, and spatial forms, as in mime: stairs, arenas, benches, ropes, broad vistas. When this is done, the stage space is no longer neutral but becomes symbolic. It then has a very real effect on the dancer, forcing him to move differently, to behave in certain ways and not in others.

Improv: Safety Zone

Each of you has a safety zone, a circle about two feet in diameter. It might be a place of fun, whereas the outside area is one of drudgery, or it could be a place of relaxation, while the outside has high tension. When you're in it, you're safe, held, warm, cozy. But you're allowed to stay there only five to ten seconds, and then you must leave. It is a place to recharge. Outside there

is challenge, excitement, danger . . . of which you can only take
so much. You seek periodic rests in your safety zone. Determine for yourself the nature of your safety zone and of the
surrounding area. ⚥ Begin . . .

Repeat with a group of people in the safety zone together.
Delineate that area in some way (with masking tape, spotlight,
etc.). Together determine the nature of the safety zone.

Choreographic Study: Symbolic Space
Use a chair, or several chairs, or a platform, and make it sym-
bolize something: home, free speech platform, tower, raft, anything. Do a study using this as theme. Note the different approaches, uses, and stage placement of symbolic space.

Turning

Turning is magical, mystical, as in trance dances. By analogy it is connected to whirlpools, spirals, to the circle and all
the symbolism that it calls forth, to inclusivity and exclusiv-
ity, to the idea of infinity, of forever, of eternity. The ending
move of Marion Scott's *Mysterium* is a good example of such
symbolic implications. Two figures, a man and woman,
loosely wound around each other like vine-serpents, keep circling in place as the lights slowly fade. We intuitively understand they are eternal.

But turning goes far beyond such symbolism. It can cause a
loss of body image; it combines fun and fright (as every child
and amusement-park-goer knows); it is disorienting. In all
these ways it has rather exceptional power as a way of moving. Part of the fascination of Laura Dean's choreography is
achieved by her extended use of spinning. To be able to over-
come dizziness in a long succession of cleanly articulated
turns truly is amazing (much as we denounce the use of physical feats per se, in dance). In doing so, the dancer defies a sort
of natural law; she surpasses the realm of the ordinary and
exists in a magical or surreal world, the world of illusion
where all things are possible.

Improv: Spinning

⟡ Close your eyes and concentrate on any ongoing image (a tornado, whirlpool, vortex, the sound "om," the spinning of the earth). Keeping this in mind, open your eyes and put one arm out in front of you. Look at your hand as you begin spinning. The spinning need not be rapid, but your speed should remain constant unless or until the spinning impels you to change. Let it continue for a good while. If you become dizzy, go with the dizziness and see what sort of movement results, or push past the dizziness by continuing to turn. Allow whatever happens to happen; let it find its own outcome.

Note and discuss how it made you feel, physically in terms of spatial orientation, sense of gravity or levity, relationship to environment or other people, to things in the room. (The impact and power of spinning on the soma-psyche is heightened the more one repeats this exercise. It is, in a way, a learned skill, and it is only by practice that one gets past the dizziness and becomes able to experience the other levels of awareness that turning can produce.)

Turning can be explored in all three planes, as Laban categorized: (1) in the vertical plane around the sagittal axis, as with cartwheels; (2) in the horizontal plane around the vertical axis of the body as with pirouettes, or other standing or sitting turns or spins, or with rolls, as when lying down; and (3) in the sagittal plane, around the horizontal axis, as with somersaults. Dance uses (2) most frequently, whereas acrobatics and gymnastics use (1) and (3). Any of them, of course, can be coupled with elevation or traveling to provide greater variety and excitement. The spectacular Russian jump is a cartwheel executed on the horizontal, or table plane, parallel to the ground. Leans, assorted body designs, shapes, changes of speed, impulse, size, and other variations can be added to any standard turn. They give the natural power inherent in turning an even stronger choreographic impact. Although turning is powerful, be cautious of the attitude, "When in doubt, turn."

(Louis Horst used to grumble about "too many turns and too much doubt" back in the days when he was teaching composition at Juilliard.)

Improv: Presenting . . . The Three Dolls!

Jumeau, the world's greatest doll-maker, is at the World's Fair. He is demonstrating his newest invention, lifelike dolls that turn. The three dolls are very jealous of each other. Each one wants to be the cleverest turning doll in the world.

ϕ The Rubber Band Doll. Twist your head as far in one direction as it will go; let it snap back to center. Twist from the waist up as far as possible, and snap back. From the feet up, and snap back. Twist with a surge of momentum that makes you pivot, on one foot, on two. Continue to explore new ways of twisting, turning, pivoting.

ϕ The Music-Box Doll. Take quick little steps in place and begin turning. Keep going around. Become involved in your turning. Vary the speeds, the shape of your arms. Play with changing directions; alternate going left and right. Let your elbow, ear, knee lead you around in the turn. Let the turn take you from very low to high, to on your toes, into the air. Travel as you turn. If you need to stop turning every so often to maintain decorum, do so but don't stop dancing. Also remember you can use very slow turns.

ϕ The Clown Doll. Turn completely in the air. Experiment with different types of somersaults, cartwheels, rolls, with sitting turns and lying down turns and kneeling turns, elbow turns and shoulder turns and heel turns, funny turns and weird turns. Try turning while you're leaning off-center, while you're falling. Dare . . . risk . . . crazy . . . scary . . . yes . . . good!

Choreographic Study: Turning

Combine a series of different turns into a short study. The featured attraction is turning; any other movement is used sparingly for the purpose of transition only. Remember the possibility of turning very slowly, and of changing directions.

Floor Pattern

The road we travel, our path in space, indicates where we are going, where we came from, and who we are. In and of itself, the path that the dancer travels is a contributing factor to the dance. Different floor patterns can be used to create different effects.

In our discussion of design, we touched on curved and straight floor patterns and their implications. One of the more distinctive spatial patterns is the circle. When used for large groups of people, as in children's games and in folk dances, the circle has great strength. The power is mainly for the participants—the unity it provides is all-encompassing—but it can also be used with an audience in mind because the power can be projected and transmitted.

Improv: Group Circle Add-In

The participants stand in large circle, more than an arm's length apart. One person starts low and runs into center, sweeping hands up to high overhead, and then returns to starting place, low. She goes in again and another person joins her. The move "to the center and out again" is repeated, adding more people each time, until everyone is doing it together. Voice, vocal sounds may be used if desired. Once the whole group is involved, let the improv find and take its own direction.

In the foregoing improv the circle, as a geometric configuration, was used to establish and build a sense of unity among a group of people. A soloist who travels in a circular path capitalizes on another powerful aspect of the circle: it symbolizes the infinite, with no beginning, and no end. There is a hypnotic quality to a path that goes round and round but never arrives. It's as if the repetition wears a groove in the earth.

The spiral has a hypnotic quality, but it also implies change and a possible end. When spiraling out, it can either arrive at some point or continue on to infinity. When it spirals in, it is completed when the center of the circle becomes the center of the dancer's body, or it may be resolved by the dancer turning (pivoting) unceasingly, eternally, in the self-contained space.

Geometric floor patterns with straight lines and angles create interest through the directness of the line and the snappiness of a sharply turned corner, resulting in a new direction, feeling, or facing.

Exploratory Work

Draw a series of distinctive floor patterns, curved and straight. Write images, dramatic situations, characterizations that seem to go with such standard patterns as the circle, the zigzag, spiral, or staircase, and others that would more appropriately make use of free forms.

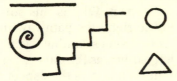 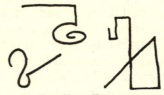

Standard Patterns   Free-Form Patterns

Figure 2

Improv: Spiral

One at a time, starting from the perimeter of the studio, do an extensive spiral inward. Use your own image, one suggested by the path of a spiral, to give your spiral a face of its own. Determine for yourself the speed, your attitude, what the center point of the spiral is about, and how you respond to it. Repeat, spiraling out. (A similar improv may be done with any of the standard patterns.)

Short & to the Point.

Pick any two floor patterns. Take a traveling movement and do it in each of the two patterns. How are they different? Do this with several contrasting locomotor movements.

Choreographic Study: Floor Pattern
Create a study in which the floor pattern is very precise and distinctive and contributes to the total effect and intention of the piece.

Stage Space

The actual physical area, the stage or arena that contains the dance, has connotations all its own. There are certain places on the stage that are stronger, others that are intimate. Stage placement, in relation to the audience, needs to be considered along with the floor patterns contained and executed within the stage space. The famous diagonal from upstage right to downstage left is so often used because it makes the most powerful visual and psychological impact. Why is this so? It moves the audience's eye from left to right, the pathway universally followed by human beings in visual scanning (even in cultures who read from right to left). It brings the dancer from a point of distance to one of proximity. It allows the dancer to cover the greatest possible distance onstage in a straight, direct path. In ballet the other diagonal—up-left to down-right— is preferred because it allows the movement to be performed to the dancer's right, which usually is the stronger side.

Theater people are acutely aware of the innuendoes of stage placement. Upstaging another actor is a prime example. Such a device is countered by the fact that, generally speaking, action takes on greater significance as it moves farther downstage, getting closer to, entering, and even impinging on the audience's space, thereby demanding their attention. Traditionally, down-left is the place for scenes of intimacy, and up-left is a weaker area to be used for moments and situations of less importance. Analysis of projective drawing tests indicates, however, that left is associated with the past and right with the future (a fact probably related to the visual scanning patterns discussed above). As seen by the audience, time progresses from stage right to stage left; this occurs at a subliminal level. The best place to convey a sense of the present is thus stage center, since it is the boundary between past and future. Down-center couples this with proximity, imparting an unmistakable sense of "here and now" for powerful, direct, audience confrontation; in both time and space, closeness is equivalent to immediacy. While placement on different areas of the stage influences the way the movement is seen, the major factors determining the strongest area are: where the dancer is, whether she is moving, where others onstage are focusing (by pointing, visual attention, or body facing), and where the light is.

Stage placement furthermore contributes to optical perspective. The contrast between a very tall and a very short dancer is evident when we place them side by side; maximized if we put the larger dancer downstage and the smaller one upstage; minimized if we bring the short one close to the audience and leave the tall dancer at the cyclorama. This demonstrates how stage placement can affect changes in perspective.

Exploratory Work

List possible images, dramatic situations, and reasons for traveling the Powerful Diagonal (from upstage right to downstage left). Are there different ones for starting down-left and going to up-right?

Improv: The Powerful Diagonal

Improvise along the up-right to down-left diagonal, using its power to the fullest. Take time to establish yourself before you start and be sure to have a definite ending when you reach down-left. This improv is to be done one at a time, but organized such that as one person finishes, another dancer is in position up-right ready to begin. The dancer may choose whether to begin and end onstage or in the wings. Those not dancing or getting ready to go on should sit in front and be the audience. Repeat the improv in reverse; begin down-left and leave, travel, or retreat to up-right. Discuss.

Choreographic Study: Stage Placement
Compose a short study where you spend most of your time
stage center or downstage left, using its full potential. Keep in
mind the effect made by how you approach and leave the prin-
cipal spot. After you show the study in the place it was intended for, restage it in a different place (center-right or up-left)
and see if, indeed, the impact is changed for the audience.
Feedback from the spectators in this exercise is crucial.

Many choreographers and directors adhere to these principles of staging, but others do not. Merce Cunningham often
chooses to ignore them in keeping with his philosophy of the
simultaneous, rather than hierarchical, importance of artistic
elements. Because he treats all elements equally, the establish-
ment of priorities becomes the responsibility of the viewer.
This democratization is a theatrical equivalent of the field
painting of artists like Jackson Pollock.

Personal Space

In everyday life, man unconsciously structures the space
around him. What is immediately surrounding him is personal and reserved for intimacy; it constitutes the private
bubble he carries around with him. For some, that space is
huge; for others, quite constricted. Intrusion into this personal
space by an outsider causes "fight or flight" unless protected
by rules or customs, as in social dancing and wrestling. Edward Hall, in *The Silent Language* and *The Hidden Dimension*, has written extensively on this subject. But there are
times when two individuals' personal space deliberately becomes one for awhile, as for mother and child, or lovers.

In dance, as in theater, private space is constantly being
exaggerated or violated by the choreographer for artistic ends.
The result may intrude on the space of the dancer-as-private-
individual. However, this intrusion is part of the choreographer's poetic license. The same two dancers who intimately
share space while executing a given movement do not neces-

sarily relate in those terms outside the studio. Young choreographers, unconsciously applying comfortable and socially acceptable spatial norms, tend to use mid-range as they position and manipulate their dancers. One must cultivate the realization that by using extremes, art rises above the commonplace, has an impact, and thus makes its statement. So we resist the usual space determinants and rules. We put body on duplicate body, like onion skins. We set intimate moments a stage span apart, as in John Butler's *After Eden* when Eve responds to the energy impact of Adam's movement from across the stage, twenty or more feet away.

The choreographer is forever dealing with space bubbles, but only in dramatic pieces does he deal with their interpersonal significance. In nondramatic pieces considerations of the space around a dancer and the distance between dancers are manipulated as any other element of the craft. Whether for visual impact or character development these factors influence movement and posture as well as the spatial relationships between dancers.

A solid close mass of bodies can evoke positive feelings ("in unity there is strength") or fearful ones (a threatening crowd). At other times, a tightly packed group can become uncomfortable for participants or observers as the personal bubbles are being squeezed, rubbed, and agitated, and that private space is being invaded.

Exploratory Work: Closing In

Next time you are talking to someone, note the distance between you that has been quite naturally arrived at. Then move away a little bit while continuing the conversation. Does it feel different? Does your friend adjust the distance? After reestablishing the comfortable distance, move in closer. How does that feel? What happens now? Try this exact same experiment with another person whose relationship to you is very different (your boss rather than your subordinate, a store clerk instead of your mom). Compare and contrast the responses in the two situations. Discuss.

Improv: Second Skin Shadowing
Similar to the Mirroring Improv (p. 20) this is done in pairs. As the name implies, one person leads while his partner works behind as his shadow. Experiment with working so closely that the shadow actually becomes a second skin to her partner, the entire front of her body touching the back of his. Experiment at different levels. Try moving across the space. As the sun sinks, the shadow lengthens, and grows farther and farther away. Continue to feel the unity and connection with your partner even though you become widely separated. At some point, switch roles, allowing the transition to occur naturally. Allow the situation to resolve itself of its own accord.

Choreographic Study: Spatial Relationships
With a partner, jointly choreograph a study using only spatial extremes. Do not limit yourselves to doing the exact same movements, as in the preceding improvisation. Perhaps turn some standard spatial conventions topsy-turvy, for example, hug, shake hands, or tickle while you are widely separated, or try throwing or having a shouting movement conversation up close.

Environment

Where you dance is obviously important. Sometimes you need to block out externals such as noisy stagehands; at other times, the environment is an integral part of the dance and affects how you move. It is a good idea to get experience in different environments, first, because dancers must be able to adjust quickly to a variety of stage types and sizes, and secondly, because unusual environments provide a rich source for extending the arena of dance as a performing art.

Dancers find themselves performing in places as diverse as high school gyms, church sanctuaries, opera houses. The suitability, plausibility, and adaptability of each separate dance to that space must be considered. A spacing run-through is obviously a necessity. The choreographer may need to make all sorts of choreographic adjustments, including new entrances and exits—"What do you mean, there's no cyc or back crossover?"

An incredible number of dances can be inspired by environments, from the ordinary to the bizarre: playground, sculpture gallery, church altar or abandoned chapel, the beach, a gymnasium or weight room. These can either be performed on location, filmed, and used afterward for conventional staging, or function merely as sources of inspiration. Don't think only of found environments such as these, but try creating your own. It's more fun than a barrel of dancers. Cover the floor with Ping-Pong balls, balloons; lace the place with Saran Wrap; build a jungle gym set with ladders, chairs, cardboard boxes; get a parachute (a time-worn idea maybe, but still useful for a formative experience). Even though these are fun, they demand careful attention to keep the movement from becoming secondary or superficial.

> *Improv/Choreographic Study: Environments*
> Choose one of the above environments or create one of your own, and . . . improvise. Keep an awareness of the space in which you're moving—the floor, walls, ceiling; the temperature, time of day, sounds; the privacy or lack thereof. All these contribute to how you move and how you feel about moving in that space. Choreograph a study that capitalizes on that particular environment.

Sometimes you have an audience all around the dancers. What usually happens when you're faced with a theater-in-the-round is that you rearrange your proscenium dance for it. For a change, why don't you *start* with a 360° audience-dancer relationship? What ideas beg to be in-the-round, communicating from every angle to inquiring, appraising eyes?

> *Choreographic Study: Dance in the Round*
> Choreograph a study that, from its conception, is oriented to the theater-in-the-round, such as "Life Is a Merry-Go-Round," "Exposed," "A Million Eyes Are Watching Me," a ritual capitalizing on the use of circle, spiral, or square as basic floor patterns, a spinning dance.

6 /
Time

Time as flow. Time as order. It
   evaporates during involvement, pleasure;
      stagnates during worry, waiting, pain;
         teases in anticipation;
            freezes in design (sculpture and painting);
               fragments in dreams and memories. Time as an
ordering force provides a matrix within which things can be
coordinated, measured, and calculated. When allowed to, it
can dictate and control in an arbitrary, predetermined, nonre-
sponsive way.

   The pulse of the people is like a barometer of their feelings;
the tempo of a group reflects their drive; their rhythms often
reflect their style. The choreographer has all of these as his
tools. The combination of them is what distinguishes different
styles of dance, such as flamenco, Balinese, jazz. The pulse of
the townspeople in Charles Weidman's *Lynchtown* and of the
Furies in Martha Graham's *Night Journey* show how they can
be put to powerful use.

Tempo

   The beat goes fast . . .
   The beat goes very slowly . . .
The speed of the beat is the tempo. It can determine, or be

determined by, the response and attitude of the dancer. A rapid tempo could cause her to rush, withdrawing in fear or conflict, or be excited in a frenzy, or dazzle with quickness as in a multiple-beat jump or when spinning in full control. The slow beat could be indulged in with sensuous pleasure or gentle caring, or could underline fatigue, pain, or sorrow.

Improv: Tempo
There are many kinds of fast tempi—very fast, medium fast, and so on. There are also many reasons to be fast—you are late, hysterical, afraid, or you love moving fast, in control or maybe even out of control. ♦ Pick what you want and play with it. Take time to experiment with different kinds of fast, and different motivations for fast. After you've explored and experimented in the realm of fast for a while, and have a handle on it, do the same with slow. There are some days it just feels good to go slowly, to indulge oneself in the pleasure of a slow stretch, a languid movement. Slowness can be soothing or it can drag us down in depression, hurt, sadness. Use the images you choose and work with it . . . slowly. Try several different moods and attitudes toward slow.

Momentum

M o m e n t u m comes to the beat . . .
When the tempo constantly increases (*accelerando*) or decreases (*ritardando*), it produces intriguing phenomena which can be used effectively in choreography. Increasing speed has its uses (a chase, the building intensity of a fight, or the simple speeding up of a movement or phrase repeated many times). It has produced many a flashy, tour de force ending. Slowing, winding down, or dying out can also provide endings, weakenings, or contrasting preludes to high points.

Momentum has an implicit affinity for energy, coupling acceleration with a raising of energy and deceleration with a lowering of it. In the following improvs we both use the affinities and juxtapose them.

Short & to the Point

Try a movement starting slow and strong; as you get faster become weaker and more gentle.

Improv: Macy's Balloon

As you work with the image in this improv, try to keep the *accelerando* and *ritardando* gradual and even.

♦ You find your body enormous, tall, heavy, bloated like an oversized Macy's parade balloon. Explore these new sensations and your new body's way of moving. Gradually your body loses some of its air. Ahh, it feels good to move with ease again. Feel the freedom of it as you return to normal size. Uh oh! That which made you oversized is coming again. You notice it approaching. You start to flee from it. It's coming at you faster and faster, starting to overtake you. You run in panic, try to shake it off, throw it away, escape. You're frantic. It's almost caught up with you, but you won't give in. You try to avoid it by moving every part of your body as fast as you can, as if your own speed could avert the occurrence. But it prevails, and gradually, bit by bit, seeps into your body and takes over. You blow up and out, bigger than self, bigger than life. Joints become bloated and stiff. Your movement is inhibited, but still you resist. You push, you tense against what is happening to your body. You're furious but almost immobile. Find some way to resolve the image.

Choreographic Study: Tempo and Accelerando/Ritardando

Create a short study that includes fast/slow and *accelerando/ ritardando*.

Duration

The beat goes on and serves as a measure . . .

The length of a movement is basically determined by how long it takes to do it. Often kinesthetic necessity determines the possible range of duration (runs and jumps can only be so slow and balances so long). Within that range a decision can be made to determine the exact duration wanted, that is, the relationship of the movement to the beat—how many beats at a given tempo the movement takes. Some movements allow little leeway; others are more flexible, and while they may require some adjustments, they also may provide new nuances as the time span changes.

Improv: Elastic Time

Divide into small groups and set a movement phrase that takes exactly ten seconds to execute. Let one group perform their phrase while the rest watch. One of the watchers acts as the clock and, standing where she's visible to all the dancers, uses her arm as the second-hand, "ticking off' the actual passage of time. The dancers repeat their phrase in twenty seconds, in thirty or in five seconds. Try it again, but expand and contract it in different ways, not uniformly slower or faster but (for instance) do the first part in regular time and then race through the end in order to finish within the shortened time limit, or the same timing, but with pauses (at expected or unexpected places), or many sections of faster and slower with none at the original timing. Switch so everyone has a chance to show and work with theirs and everyone has the opportunity to watch the results and changes that occur.

Choreographic Study: Elastic Time

Using the possibilities presented in the improv, set a study based on one movement phrase repeated at varying lengths.

Clock Time

Tic/toc/the/beat/goes/on . . .

The clock—servant and master—keeps our complex world going and frustrates us in the process. Clock time is often restrictive because it simply doesn't allow for individual differences, natural timing, or chance occurrences. In dance, it need not be so restrictive. Freedom can be gained by opening up internal structures within given, limited quantities of time. If you have three minutes of uncounted choreographic movement, you can dance according to your own kinesthetic timing (for instance, you do not have to land on a specific beat after the balance but can indulge in the balance, holding it as long as you want). Using the clock as structure in this way actually allows for flexibility and therefore presents new opportunities for choreographic ingenuity. It's fun to test your perception of time. Do you really know how long a minute is? (Try it out—it'll only take a minute.)

> *Improv: The Whimsical Minute, Version I*
> The point of this improv is best made when done in a group. One person serves as the timer. when she says "Go," move very slowly for your perception of one minute. Move with a sense of hovering, sluggishness, daydreaming, or indulgence. Freeze when you think one minute has elapsed. The timer should note how many seconds the briefest and the longest perception of one minute lasts.
> Repeat as above, except this time move very rapidly for what you sense to be one minute, with a sense of haste, urgency. Again, the responses are timed. Afterward, the timer should announce how long the shortest and longest minute took, for both the slow movement and the rapid movement. No names, please, this isn't a contest! Discuss your perceptions. (This is an expandable exercise—see Version II on p. 76)

Yes, time seems to have a life of its own. It can feel endless if you are waiting for it to pass (or if using sixty seconds to complete one développé into arabesque), or it can pass without notice when you are excitedly involved. The clock will tell you the actual time of a sequence, but what you do choreographically determines how the time is perceived and how it will make the audience feel.

Regular/Irregular

beat, beat, beat,   beat, beat,   beat,   beat . . .
A regular beat can be supportive and comforting (rocking a

baby to sleep) or monotonous and deadening. It's good for relaxing and dancing to (dinner music, waltzes). It's especially helpful in partner and group work where it functions as a unifying force, keeping everyone's timing synchronized. Marches and work songs take advantage of its effect in this way.

When the beat is irregular, things get unpredictable. There is no constant element to lean back on. It's hard to teach, record, anticipate, and accompany. But it can be fun, a challenging, intellectual game in which you are continuously making decisions. In an improvisational situation, some people find it initially annoying (it's definitely more difficult), but when they work it through, it usually opens new doors as they perceive the possibilities and power of irregular timing. As a compositional tool, the choreographer can utilize its jarring, disjointed, surprising, annoying, or comic effects in a variety of ways.

Exploratory Work
As you work through this chapter and get acquainted with tempo, accent, meter, rhythm, make a list of regular and irregular examples of each.

Accent

BEAT, beat, beat, BEAT, beat, beat . . .
An accent is an emphasis or stress. (For other ways of achieving emphasis, see pp. 107–08.) The place where the accent falls regularly tends to feel like the starting point. This is probably related to the way impulse functions and the feeling it produces (see pp. 24–25).

Short & to the Point
Clap **1** 2 3, **1** 2 3, **1** 2 3 continuously; then change the accent to 1 **2** 3, 1 **2** 3, 1 **2** 3; after a while you will begin to feel it as **2** 3 1, **2** 3 1, **2** 3 1, showing how we unconsciously equate accent with impulse and impulse with beginnings.

Try the above in movement. Do a series of triplets (down, up, up) to **1** 2 3. Then try beginning the triplet on the up—up, down, up—to the same meter (**1** 2 3). What happens when you try to change it in this way?

Improv: Hypnotized

With drum or clapping, etc., provide a slow, steady, even tempo. Allow time for each instruction to be realized. ϕ Hypnotize someone by moving on each beat and only on the beat, using different parts of the body. Become hypnotized yourself. Move as in a trance. Keep the steady beat. Every so often accent the movement in some special way (bigger, stronger). Now accent the first of every four counts (3, 4, **1**) . . . now the first of every three (2, 3, **1**) . . . and now of every two (2, **1**). [Drum softly returns to the steady unaccented pulse.] Now move only between the beats. Move at random—anywhere, anytime—on or off the beat, a couple in a row, wait nine, whatever, moving the accents around.

As you continue moving, let the random timing carry you out of the trance. What images come from moving in a random way? Let the randomness and the movements become more and more erratic. Do the images go toward comedy or toward the bizarre? Work with them. [The drum never stopped beating; it just stopped accenting.] Move again with the steady beat. Leave out a beat every so often. Freeze! Don't go dead! Leave out two, three, six beats in a row, but have the held position antcipate what's coming or remind us of what was. Keep the beat, the timing, going on internally while you are frozen. Mix long and short rests. Bring it to an end.

[Possibly have half the group sit and watch while the others move. You may want to let the watchers take turns providing the drum beat. This helps give practice in maintaining a steady pulse, because there is a tendency to speed up.]

Discuss regular accents, syncopation (any deliberate upsetting of the normal pulse, meter, accent, rhythm), random relationship of movement to the beat, and use of rests.

Agogic accent is a special type of accent that is wholly the result of duration (discussed above, pp. 60–61). The simple fact that one note lasts a different amount of time from all of the notes surrounding it (these being of equal duration), creates the feeling of accent. For instance, when one long note is preceded (or followed) by a series of short ones (as in the major motif of the first movement of Beethoven's Fifth Symphony), that's sufficient by itself to make the longer note the accented one, even with absolutely no other differentiation (such as dynamics or pitch). Try this out for yourself, with anything as simple as a side-to-side movement of the forearm, and it will be immediately apparent.

Meter

beat 2 3 4, beat 2 3 4, . . .

When an accent occurs at regular periodic intervals, meter is produced, for meter is the grouping of beats around an accent: **1** 2, **1** 2, **1** 2, or **1** 2 3, **1** 2 3. This establishes a regularity in timing. It provides a predictable structure that supports and propels the movement. Meter can be a constant to play off of and to contrast against.

Some movements because of their natural kinesthetic timing demand certain rhythms. For instance, in a regular swing the suspension will last twice as long as the drop; because of this natural subdivision into threes, the swing movement usually occurs in a 3/4 meter.

Choreographic Study: The Essence of Movement
in Different Meters

Sing threes to yourself, any tempo, and find a movement that has the feeling of threes. Repeat with fours. Discuss and define what the essence of moving in threes is all about and how it differs from fours. Are there any specific movement affinities that you notice? Set a study in which you use two or three different meters. Pay attention to the affinity of the movement for the chosen meter. Be sure that the change from one meter to the other is clear.

Short & to the Point

In each of the following examples, try to keep the essence of the movement while attending clearly to the meter.

1. Do a triplet in 4/4.
2. Do a march in 6/8.
3. Do a full body swing in 5/4; in 4/4 with two counts drop and two counts suspension, then with one count drop and three counts suspension.
4. Find a movement that is repeatable. Determine its meter. Accommodate it to another meter, then another. What new things do you find about the movement with each accommodation?

Some meters, in and of themselves, are uneven and can be used to produce a sense of tension or comedy. The physicality of moving unevenly is inherently different from moving evenly, ofttimes resulting in a one-sided or limping effect. In 5/4 meter the classic secondary accent occurs on 3 or 4 (**1** 2 **3** 4 5 or **1** 2 3 **4** 5). But in it, as in others such as 7/4 or 9/4, the secondary accent(s) can stress any of the various beats: **1** 2 3 **4 5** 6 7, **1** 2 3 4 **5** 6 7, and so on.

Improv: 5/4

[Have a drum or other accompaniment establish a moderate 5/4 with *no* secondary accent.] ϕ Listen to the drum beat. In your mind, count out five and start accenting two beats, 1 and 3 or 1 and 4. Try stepping it—down on the accented beats and up on the others. Sense the choppiness, how lop-sided it is. Now, while remaining in place, start moving other body parts only on the accents. What images come to mind? Alternate at will between stationary and traveling, but keep the integrity of the accent constant. Try to make the shorter one abrupt and sharp in contrast to the sustained longer one, giving each a different character. Get any comic or slapstick effects? A clown? Chasing mosquitoes? Work with the images. [Drum fades out.] Let each dancer use the timing he needs to work out his image. Discuss images and resulting movements.

Choreographic Study: 7/4
Set a short piece in 7/4 timing. Vary the secondary accents.
   Discussion. Note that once a regular accent is established,
no matter *how* uneven, it becomes predictable.

Other ways of creating interest and complexity in accents
are: (1) with the use of a movement accent that does not coincide with a sound accent; (2) through random placement of a
new accent; (3) by creating an interesting and more complex
pattern, such as **1** 2 3, 1 **2** 3, 1 2 **3;** or (4) with the use of a
second voice, in which the effect is cumulative and the degree
of intensity of the accents is additive, producing an overall
rhythmic pattern:

Voice I: **1** 2 3 **1** 2 3 **1** 2 3   **1**   2   3 (a sound or movement in 3/4)
Voice II: **1** 2 3 4 **1** 2 3 4 **1**   2   3   4 (a sound or movement in 4/4)
           ①2 3 **4 5** 6 **7 8 9 10** 11 12

Improv: Paired Meters
[Improvised in pairs to an agreed upon basic tempo.] Dancer A
works in 3/4 time, using up-and-down movement. Dancer B,
circling Dancer A, works in 4/4 using in-and-out movement,
and related to Dancer A.

Sometimes referred to as *resultant rhythm*, this layering effect builds texture and volume in movement and sound, creating a powerful environment that can envelop the dancer and
audience. Vocal choruses use this with electrifying results, as
in Orff's *Carmina Burana* and Stravinsky's Symphony of
Psalms. A brilliant use of this same technique in dance is
Humphrey's *Passacaglia and Fugue* to the music of Bach.

Natural Rhythms

   the natural beat . . . thump, thump, thump
Man is involved in many rhythmic patterns. While all of them

have roots in the body, some are carried out by the autonomic nervous system (such as breath, heartbeat) while others result from repetitive physical actions (threshing wheat, rowing a boat, jogging). Natural rhythms, intrinsic to man's functioning and perception, are an integral part of art. They affect the dancer (or the character being portrayed) and the audience in many subtle and obvious ways. When the dance is composed before the music, the natural rhythms (with their qualifying tempi) can be especially exploited.

Exploratory Work
Make a list of natural rhythms, both voluntary and involuntary.

Improv: Heartbeat/Rhythm Circle
[Note: This takes at least half an hour to complete and a minimum of eight people.]
Run around the room three times as fast as you can. Lie down and become very quiet. Listen to your own body. Find some pulse or a pattern that is repeating itself—it may be your heartbeat, pulse, or the inhale-exhale of your breath. Let this rhythmic pattern be reflected somewhere in your body, a finger, foot. It might be very small; that's okay. Move it to another part of your body. Keep the rhythm constant. Hear it as a steady internal voice. No matter what else you're asked to do or what else happens, this rhythm is sacred—it remains constant. Let another part of your body move to that rhythm. Let the movement get bigger, stronger, keeping the same pulse. Keep adding other parts of your body until your whole body is moving to it. Let it take you to a sitting position, to kneeling, standing. Put it only in your left hand ... your right shoulder ... your head; now into everything from your waist up. Hips only, Knees only. Everything from your ankles up. Let your feet make the rhythm. Stamp out your rhythmic pattern with your feet.

Keep your own rhythm but become aware of the others in the room as well. Start moving through the space. Start a circling of the room, counterclockwise, keeping your own rhythm in your feet and body. [Responding to the emerging group sound, the leader begins to identify and play the common rhythm on a drum, e.g., ♩ ♫ ♩. Note: If you know a good drummer, have him come in and play. Tell him that you need a clear, steady pulse, with elaboration.]

Feel your own independent rhythm growing fainter. Gradually it gives way and you give it up as you increase your sensitivity to the feel of the whole group. Listen for the rhythm of the group as the drum is beating it. Pick up on that and adjust to it. Feel it getting stronger as you put it into your feet. Let me hear you all working together. You are part of the group; you are an integral part of a group in a magic circle. Without you the circle could not exist. It is powerful, compelling. The rhythm is so strong in your feet that you do not need the drum. [Fade out the drumbeat.] Keep moving to the beat you are making.

Become aware of the center of the circle. There is something special there. Now, with movement and timing different from what you are doing, cross through the center. Only x people [designate how many] should be crossing the circle at any one time. [Adjust the number depending on the size of the group, about one-quarter or one-third works well. Drum beat comes in again for support.] Each of you should cross the center at least three times. Be sure the movement is very different rhythmically as you cross—roll on the floor, or go in slow motion.

These next times as you cross, pay particular attention to the center. Pay homage to the magic that is there. Go at least twice.

This time, pay special attention to the other people who are in the center with you. Dance with them. Take as much time as you want in the middle. There can be any number of people in the center as long as there are at least two people outside maintaining the integrity of the circle and the consistency of the rhythm. You may go in and out as you please.

[After this goes on for a while . . .] Let it go where it wants to. It may even come to a stop and start in again. Eventually, let it find its own ending.

Discussion.   How did you feel about giving up your rhythm for the group's? Did the circle or its center become important, magical? Why or why not? What was it like to go against the rhythm of the group when you were in the center? How did the ending feel?

Choreographic Study: Natural Rhythms
Create a study juxtaposing two different natural rhythms.

Stillness

the beat stops . . . pause . . .
If time is flow, it also contains its opposite, stillness, when the flow pauses. Stillness is not *inaction*. It is a waiting, with a sense of ongoingness. A hesitation, a caught breath, is a moment arrived at, held precious, and left. Stillness is gathering in the past . . . holding, savoring the present . . . anticipating the future. It contains within it both past and future. There is a hint and promise of what is to come, a memory or what was—stillness, a moment tattooed.

Stillness provides untold potential—the quiet before the storm, restful or arresting, relief or suspense—yet it is too rarely used, especially by the less experienced choreographer. Why is this? Are dancers or choreographers afraid to stop or pause because dancing is "supposed to be" about moving? Afraid to be still because art is "supposed to say something"? Afraid to be quiet because it might mean they have nothing to say?

Movement contains stillness even as yin contains yang. Sometimes to speak elegantly, you must be quiet. The fullest statement may be empty of movement; the strongest movement impact can be set off by stillness. As a dancer, if you can learn to be really still, you can move your audience.

Improv: Thawing
♀ You are frozen stiff. You begin to thaw in one part of your body and then that refreezes. Then another part thaws. As thawing occurs, memories flood in, coloring the movement that precipitated them—memories of warmth, silliness, struggling, wistfulness. Sometimes the thawing overlaps and sometimes you are completely frozen again. At times the thawing is very slow; at other times, instantaneous. Once thawed, the body part may want to try out various movements before it refreezes.

Improv: Scared Stiff

ϙ Imagine you hear something scary—a scream, crash, or eerie sound. It is ominous, petrifying, yet you need to react. You alternate between being motionless and moving, responding to the threat. Let the movement and stillness reflect what you hear: a giant monster, a roomful of snakes or snarls, hundreds of swinging clubs, flying bats, a swarm of mosquitoes. You might respond violently, cautiously, sneakily, suddenly. Play with different images that trigger different types of reaction in movement.

Stillness may be followed by an unexpected movement that surprises or startles the audience. This could have a comic effect (a series of grand, show-off leaps, a pause as in preparation for more with the music building, the dancer ready, and then a collapse to a crumpled heap on the floor). The device of unexpected change could also be used dramatically to reveal a new aspect of a character or a sudden change in a situation.

Choreographic Study: "Don't just do something—be there!"
Create a study where stillness takes on a primary role. You can choose whether or not to use drama, comedy, or unexpectedness as part of your motivation. As you work, assess each moment of stillness that you have choreographed. Look at each as though it is a piece of sculpture, a tableau. Carefully determine how long you will hold the stillness (perhaps some for just a split second, perhaps all for the same length of time, perhaps not). Know, kinesthetically or cognitively, why you are holding each position for that prescribed length of time. *Make the stillnesses mean.* Use them to capture the eye of your audience.

7 /
Energy

In dance, it's the energy that provides the *go power*. Underneath the airborne leap, the held arabesque, the fall-roll-suspension is the muscle flow of the dancer's body . . . energy.

Terminology for this, last of the three basic elements of dance, is as vague as it is widespread. In dealing with energy, people use a variety of words to refer to almost the same thing. Let's begin then, by clarifying *our* definitions for the purposes of this book. *Energy*, *force*, *dynamics*, and *qualities* are all sloppily used terms. The fact that they are used interchangeably results in a confusion of what the words mean and what the "things" are that they supposedly refer to. It prevents a precision in thinking about and perceiving them, and therefore in applying them. It matters less which word is chosen than that we consistently use a specific word to convey a specific concept and can therefore communicate with greater precision.

This is how we'll use the following words:

Energy is the potential for force, the capacity for action and for overcoming resistance or gravity. As an element of dance, it is a pure entity in the same way that space and time are.

Force has to do with the magnitude or intensity of the energy exerted, expended, or released. Force exists on a continuum that ranges from strong to gentle. Laban uses *weight*, in Effort/Shape, as a near equivalent to *force*.

Dynamics is an interaction of force with time—the two playing together. It results in action in the body. Every movement is dynamic—it exists over time and has been achieved by using force.

Movement Qualities are the distinctly observable attributes or characteristics produced by dynamics and made manifest in movement. For example, the dynamic coupling of strong with fast results in a sharp or whipping quality, while the coupling of gentle and slow produces a melting or free-floating quality.

Energy (active/passive)

Until energy is actualized, until it is used or released, it is like a ticking bomb. At the moment when energy is expended to *any* degree by or on a mass (a body) across time and space, it becomes force and produces movement. Force can be self-induced or it can be the result of an external power, in which case it becomes reactive. For example: Two people are on-stage. One is stage center, a tranquil statue, frozen in time and space. The other is a light, bright, and highly spirited dancer, charging, whirling, leaping about the stage as dancers are wont to do. Suddenly she runs plumb into the statue. ZONK!! Stunned by the impact, she reels away. But the statue has remained motionless, in exactly the same position, still as stone. In this story, try to identify the use of energy, force, dynamics, and movement qualities. Has force been used by either of the characters, and if so how, when, and by whom? If it seems appropriate—or if, for instance, you failed to realize that the statue was exerting force initially (simply to defy gravity) and increased her use of force at the moment of impact (in order to keep from reacting)—try it.

Since energy is potential, one can choose whether or not to use it. Active and passive are not components of force, for they speak to *whether or not* energy is exerted (like an on–off switch), not to *how much* force is used (like a dimmer switch).

When active, we are employing force, whether against gravity, self, an object, or another body. When passive, we are foregoing our energy potential, choosing to give ourselves over to natural or man-made forces acting upon us. Gravity is one of these ever-present forces. There is no way we can move, much less dance, and not take it into account. While gravity influences everything we do, it is most obvious in collapsing, jumping, swinging, and falling. It also has an immediate influence on climbing and balancing.

Short & to the Point: Jelly-Jointed

This is done in trios while some of the group watches. One person is jelly-jointed (rubber-boned, in a state of collapse); the other two people have the task of trying to stand him up.

Discussion. Talk about the passivity/activity observed. Was the one dancer totally collapsed, passive, a blob? What was his relationship to gravity? How does active energy deal with gravity? Discuss a swing in terms of gravity. Can you think of possible situations in which a person is passive and does not use energy? What are some of the connotations of passive/active energy?

Force (strong/gentle)

By our definition, all force (no matter how strong or gentle) is active and is realized in movement. Remembering that strength and gentleness are simply categories and include no subjective value judgments, let's look at some possible positive and negative ideas about them.

	Strong	Gentle
Positive	bold, authoritative, dominant, powerful, controlling, aggressive	soft, adaptable, pliable, subtle, caring
Negative	inflexible, hard, tough, stubborn, blatant	submissive, weak, mindless, wishy-washy, malleable

It's all in how you look at it. The choreographic implications are obvious.

The amount of force used will affect the quality and substance of any given movement. The dramatic implications of force are apparent. Perhaps less apparent is how the use of force in nondramatic pieces can be aesthetically intriguing in and of itself (just as the mathematical manipulations of space and time, or as "form for form's sake" is).

We, as a culture, are particularly attuned to strength, power, and aggression. Indeed, these would be primary characteristics of our national movement style according to movement behavior analysis. Modern dance, born and raised in this culture, also stresses these qualities. This is not to say that gentle (or soft) movement isn't used in modern dance, and successfully so, yet it tends to be used in smaller amounts, as a contrasting element to strength (thus making the strong appear even stronger). It requires heightened finesse in composition to make it work and capture the eye and imagination of the audience. The Western eye simply isn't partial to, doesn't have the predisposition for, the subtlety and softness that the Eastern eye does; it isn't as receptive to the variety and nuance available in lightness and detail. For this reason, much of the Japanese Noh theater eludes us. (Even when their action becomes lively and fast the energy is contained; there is a certain restraint; sobriety prevails.) Because we are less inclined to see in that way, we are less inclined to create in or even appreciate that mode.

An American audience finds it difficult to watch Robert Wilson's *Prologue to Deaf Man's Glance* in which sustained movement is used to enact a short scene so slowly that the movement is barely noticeable. The degree of force is absolutely constant throughout, monotone. The climax, a psychologically disturbing and intense moment in which a man comes to knife a sleeping child, is achieved via dramatic inevitability rather than through any change in, or eruption of, energy. Some people have similar difficulty with Ann Halprin's *Procession*. Both of these pieces have few, if any, changes in dynamics; neither of them overtly uses great amounts of physical force.

Although strength has been emphasized in American dance, both ends of the force continuum have been (and need to be) choreographically explored. There's the mad scene in *Giselle* and the soft, light breathlessness of *The Dying Swan*. Erick Hawkins's *Here and Now with Watchers*, with its flowing calm, is on one end of the spectrum, while Alvin Ailey's "Move Members, Move" from *Revelations* is an example of the other. The ability to manipulate consciously and intuitively the whole spectrum of force is crucial for the choreographer.

Exploratory Work

Make a list of characteristics and actions inherent in the categories "strong" and "gentle."

Improv: The Whimsical Minute, Version II

This is the expanded version of the improv on page 62. Repeat this improv with these added energy qualifiers.

Move in slow motion for your perception of a minute (1) with a lot of strength—twisting like a corkscrew into the stubborn cork of a wine bottle, or pressing against an imaginary wall to make the room larger; (2) gently, with very little strength—drifting aimlessly through outer space, or hang-gliding down to some predetermined landing patch.

Move very rapidly for one minute, either using (1) a lot of force—caught in the middle of the street, dodging traffic from all directions, or smashing one blood-thirsty mosquito after another; (2) just a whisper of force—flitting from one thing to another as a butterfly flits from petal to bud, or quickly flicking a thousand balloons with different parts of your body one after another, lightly into the air.

Discussion. Which of the four variations makes you most kinetically aware of creating tension in the body? What changes occur in the use of space when you increase the force? How does moving fast or slow influence your perception of a minute? How does your perception of a minute change with alterations in the use of force?

Choreographic Study: Force
Working in pairs, create a short study in which each of you takes on a predetermined amount of force as part of your character or movement motif. Have an interaction with one another based on that.

Movement Qualities: Dynamics in Action

Dynamics

Dynamics is an abstraction, a concept that couples force with time and produces a more complex, but nevertheless theoretical, entity of its own. Therefore, we cannot deal in movement with dynamics per se, but rather must deal with its progeny, qualities.

If dynamics is the abstraction, then qualities are the tangible forms this abstraction takes in the physical body. It is the manifestation of time and force produced by the body as it moves. Movement qualities can be categorized as Valerie Hunt does (into burst, undulate, sustained, and vibratory), or they can be the grand umbrella under which every type of movement from apelike to zigzagging falls.[1]

Movement Qualities

The term *qualities* has been used for years in discussing and defining movement. You can find lists and lists of them in books on creative dance for children. But for the very finest, most comprehensive list of all, we refer you to the section on motion in *Roget's International Thesaurus of English Words and Phrases*, edited by C. D. Sylvester Mawson (New York: Thomas Crowell Co., 1935). Given the material in that and other dance books, you have plenty to go from, and it would be redundant for us to make such lists here.

Exploratory Work
How many *movement quality* words can you think of? It is less important that every word be truly a movement quality

than that the cogs have been set in motion and you're thinking in terms of movement qualifiers. You can also have a list of potential quality sources—images such as popcorn, a vise, taffy, fireworks.

Improv: Qualities Change-About

Each person chooses several favorite qualities from his list. Divide into groups of four or five. The dancers take turns leading their group, calling out one quality, letting the group respond for a while, then calling out another, allowing enough response time for each quality. Repeat at a quicker pace with the dancers making abrupt or gradual changes between each quality. Alternate leaders. [Structured in this way the improv gives each member of the group a chance to lead, to observe while leading, and to participate—all of which are useful skills to develop.]

Choreographic Study: Movement Qualities

Compose a short study, using three movement qualities. Any quality may occur more than once, but none may occur more than three times. Use only the three chosen qualities; transitions must be made within a framework of one of the qualities.

Percussive/Sustained

Movement qualities fall generally into two major categories:

Percussive	Sustained
(Staccato)	(Legato)
the nature of which is "detached"	the nature of which is "smooth"
sharp starts and stops sudden, abrupt	flowing, prolonged, drawn-out, streaming

The difference between these appears relatively simple; certainly no big conceptual misunderstandings seem likely. But confusion can arise because of the tendency to see percussive and sustained as categories of time. It is particularly easy to get them mixed up with fast and slow (which, in actuality, are aspects of speed or tempo). However, percussive and sustained are concerned with how movement is initiated rather than with the *speed* at which it occurs. For instance, we can identify Pachelbel's "Canon" and Rimsky-Korsakoff's "Flight of the Bumble Bee" as both being predominantly sustained—the first is slow-paced sustained, while the second, though also sustained, is fast.

Short & to the Point

Let's try the possible ways of combining percussive and sustained with fast and slow. Respond in movement to the images given:

1. a machine gun (percussive-fast) shooting down a jet plane (sustained-fast)

2. a man with hiccups (percussive-slow) walking on the moon (sustained-slow)

3. an automatic Morse Code transmitter gone haywire, sending erratic, rapid, and infrequent messages (percussive-fast mixed with percussive-slow)

4. a speedy slithering snake (sustained-fast), then a slow, stalking snake (sustained-slow)

Another aspect of time, duration, can also cause confusion. While sustained movement has a range of duration—it can last for six seconds or sixty—percussive does not. Each individual percussive movement occurs within a single instant. Of course you could have many, many percussive movements that add up to sixty seconds. Exactly how many separate movements occur during that minute would be determined by the rate at which they were done.

The distinction, then, between percussive and sustained does not rest on time. Nor does it involve the quantitative aspects of energy. It is not the amount of energy but how it is expended that makes the difference. The expenditure of large amounts of energy in sharp, staccato spurts will result in strong, thrusting movements (i.e., percussive), whereas small amounts of energy, also applied in sharp, staccato spurts, will yield gentle, lighter movements such as flitting or flicks (again, percussive). In conjunction with sustained, high energy might produce a pushing movement, low energy a drifting one. Low energy sustained is like gently falling snow, while high energy sustained could be recognized in the strength of a tornado. Although the amount of force changes the qualitative aspects of movement, it can't make a percussive movement sustained or vice versa.

Short & to the Point

Move to each of the following images: (1) you are walking across a stream with heavy boots on, up to your neck in water—every so often a current gently lifts you up and carries you along; (2) you are slashing through a jungle with a machete while being annoyed by wisps of spider webs. Define each movement as percussive or sustained and as high or low energy. Discuss your results.*

Using all the combinations of percussive/sustained with speed (fast or slow) and with amount of energy (high or low), we have eight possible categories:

1. Percussive–Fast–High Energy
2. Percussive–Fast–Low Energy
3. Percussive–Slow–Low Energy
4. Percussive–Slow–High Energy
5. Sustained–Slow–High Energy[2]
6. Sustained–Slow–Low Energy
7. Sustained–Fast–Low Energy
8. Sustained–Fast–High Energy

Exploratory Work

Physically work out the eight categories defined above. (Why are they arranged in this particular sequence?) Find appropriate labels for each such as yank, tap, melt. Compare your movements and their names with others. For each label, make a list of images you could use with movement.

*The stream image alternated sustained high-energy with sustained low-energy; the jungle image alternated percussive high-energy with percussive low-energy.

Improv: Percussive and Sustained
Using your labels and images, try the combinations that juxtapose the extremes, such as 1 against 6, or 3 against 8. In movement, juxtapose the remaining four categories into two pairs of
opposites. Now, start with 1 and move successively through to
8. In doing this you will be working with neighboring movements, changing only one aspect each time while all the rest
remain constant.

In the realm of percussive/sustained, seemingly nothing is
simple. Sustained and percussive can occur simultaneously in
different parts of your body. A classic barre exercise in ballet
consists of staccato petits battements battus coupled with a
legato port de bras. To further complicate matters, careful
analysis of a punch with a long follow-through reveals a
movement that is initially percussive, but becomes sustained.
Or a sustained movement can change to percussive—remember the feeling of walking down the stairs in the dark and not
realizing that there was another step yet to go?

Improv: Perstained/Sucussive
You figure it out!

Choreographic Study: Pure Percussive or Pure Sustained
Pick either percussive or sustained. Create a study using only
movement of that type. To keep it from becoming boring, remember to incorporate changes in speed and in amount of energy used.

As concepts, percussive and sustained may seem complicated, confusing. Fortunately it is much easier to understand
them kinesthetically. Try using your expanded understanding
of movement qualities in a longer and more sophisticated
improv.

Improv: A Qualitative Quiet—Movement Within Stillness
For this improv you need to have one or more people drawing
for each person dancing. The emphasis is not on artistic ability

in drawing; rather it is on clarity in execution by the mover and on capturing the essential quality of the movement in the quick sketch.

The mover moves with one specific movement quality (such as ooze, squiggle, pulsate, or jab) for ten to fifteen seconds, improvising as she goes. She then lets her movements culminate in a "stillshape" that captures the essence of that movement quality. Thus, the movement leads to a position and culminates in a moment of stillness. When she freezes in the stillshape, the others quickly sketch, in pencil, the essential quality of movement that was captured within that stillness. The lines of the drawing should reflect the nature of the movement that produced the held shape: if the movement was jagged, the lines should be correspondingly sharp, jagged, angular; if the movement was lyrical and airy, the lines would be light and soft.

Each mover does a series of four to six of these; she holds her stillness for thirty seconds and then immediately begins moving with a different quality.

Discuss your sketches. [It would be interesting to repeat this improv with an art class and see their interpretations of the movement qualities.]

8 /
Forming

Form's Natural Existence and Artistic Use

Forming is as basic to art as it is to life. Form is present throughout nature, in all the forces of the universe, in all the stages of life. The laws which govern natural patterns are not arbitrary; they have a function—to keep life together—and they do so with supreme artistry, coordinating all of life and matter, from the simplest to the most complex.

All things evolve via one of a series of forms or forming devices: cycles, progressions, stages of development. Such forming or sequencing is inherent in life, from the growth of a tree, to the water cycle, to the evolution of the species, to the structure of the stars and galaxies. We can even find form in cataclysmic events, such as in the build, climax, and resolution of volcanic eruption.

Man did not invent form. Rather, out of an innate drive to make order out of chaos, to understand and make sense of the universe about him, he discovered the existence of form.

Beginning-Middle-End	birth, life, death
Idea of Climax	making love, a volcano
A B A	day, night, day
Theme and Variation	the four seasons (year after year following the same sequence, but never exactly the same)

Unity, Variety, Contrast   the human race
and so on, ad infinitum.

   Form existed, and humans conceptualized, abstracted, and
then incorporated it into their own creations, into their highest expressions about life, into art. Cycles, patterns, and form
are so much a part of life that they are understood to be part of
the definition of life itself. Form has the same inherent defini-
tional relationship with art. It provides the internal logic that
holds a piece of art together and makes it work. The effect of
form is so strong, our need and understanding of it so perva-
sive, that, as John Martin says, it "is capable of operating in
and of itself." He goes on to say that form "may be merely
that . . . abstract perfection which never ceases to titillate the
aesthetic sensitivity" and that it is possible to produce "an
aesthetic effect through form rather than through content."[1] So
form can serve dualistically—either to carry the message or be
the message itself; it can be the message or the messenger.
This is particularly true in classical art, wherein the form itself is the nexus and the goal—the intention, message, and
satisfaction. Here, one can find pleasure in abstract relationships, the way it all fits together, yielding a sense of complete-
ness and overriding unity.
   There are many forms and an infinite number of possible
realizations for any one of them (the number of possible
ABA's is obviously limitless). Learning choreography (or any
art) is learning that the forms do exist, getting acquainted with
some of them, and being open to discovering and trying out
lots of ways for using them. Arieti, in his book *Creativity: The
Magic Synthesis,* says: "There are certain underlying orderly
arrangements in everything beyond and within us. More than
the inventing of new things, creativity often implies the *discovery* of these underlying orderly arrangements."[2]
   Universal forms in nature appear in both a pure state and in
a complex, overlapping, and therefore seemingly random
state. We may lose sight of the whole, because some patterns

exist over an incredibly long span of time; it is only from an equally long-range and objective (even historical) perspective that it becomes possible to discern the form.

This is how art functions: art takes and uses these patterns and condenses them, isolates, captures, highlights, and presents them, thus distilling the form from the complex morass. This ordering of the complexity is a necessary part of what makes art important to people. Philosopher Susanne Langer carries this so far as to support the idea that nothing has an aesthetic existence without form. There is reassurance in recognizable patterns and forms—a feeling of identification, familiarity, even comfort.

Form is not external, independent—a container that some artist arbitrarily conceived, pulled together, and labeled an aesthetic must. Form existed in nature; man perceived it, and realizing its potential, its power, he capitalized on it as an elemental necessity in the creation of art. When best employed, form grows with and supports an idea, yielding an organic structure wherein the medium, message, and format all contribute to and complement one another. This yields an organic form, the concept so widely applied and accepted as a yardstick in considering the aesthetic integrity of any work of art.

For our purposes, *forming* has a dual function. It is both (1) the process of developing material, and (2) the process of giving it a structure. The first of these falls within the category of choreographic devices, while the second is subsumed under compositional structures.

Applying some of the devices and more structured forms to the actual creation of dance is rewarding because it not only gives a sense of growing knowledge and of kinship with other art forms, but it provides ways in which you can work, even in periods of noninspiration. Better yet, it results in creative work, even though its approach is (or can be) rather mechanical or cerebral.

Learning about form by attending to such traditional modes

as ABA and to such devices as motif and development involves conscious, conscientious manipulation. In traditional music composition, complete scores are written using formal structures (e.g., theme and variaton). In dance, they are utilized less for their overall structure than for creating sequences and sections within the larger work. As such, these modes will serve to sharpen your intellectual understanding of the craft, your manipulative skills, and to develop the resources at your disposal.

Although in this chapter we are dealing with the externals of devices and forms as they pertain to the content, the exercises, improvisations, and compositions are a way of developing technical skill as a choreographer. They may be thought of as the stuff that the craft feeds on, the thousand pliés, ronds de jambe, and battements of choreography!

Organic Form

There is a Zen saying, "You have allowed the cloth to weave the cloth." That is the essence of organic form. It is a term often used, seemingly intuitively understood by those who know it, but quite mysterious and elusive to those who don't.

Organic form is about the life within; it is equivalent to the characters in a novel taking on a life of their own which the novelist, in writing, obediently follows. It is like Michelangelo's idea that the form exists within the piece of marble; the sculptor's task is to chip away the extraneous matter and uncover its presence. Organic form is void of anything that hasn't grown naturally from the basic idea; it relates to natural growth patterns, like a flower that progresses from seed, to sprout, to plant, to blossom, and to seed again. It has to do with the life of a piece, how and when and where it needs to go next in order to retain its own integrity and validity of form and purpose.

In dance, it may be helpful to think in terms of the movement within the stillness (see pp. 70–71), the potential within the movement, the direction within the potential. The following two improvs, done sequentially, may help clarify this.

Improv: The Realization of a Shape
Done in trios. One person makes a shape and shows it to the others. All three start in neutral and simultaneously find their own way to flow into that shape and then out of it. Take turns creating the initial shape and watching the different ways in which it can be arrived at and embarked from.

Improv: A Life Within
◊ Design a shape. Get into it and hold it for a short while. Get in touch with how that shape feels, where the tensions are, muscularly, dramatically. What is its intent? What is the shape about? Imagine that shape is going to come to life. How would it move? Do it—come to life. Find out what the relationship is between its external design and its internal potential for movement. Experiment with radically different types of shapes— graceful ones, distorted ones, angular and soft ones, strong or weak ones—and the different lives that exist within each of them (see "Improv: A Qualitative Quiet," pp. 81–82).

Choreographic Study: A Life Within
Using a variety of shapes that can work together, create a study about the shapes and their inherent resultant movement—the life within.

Transitions

One of the earmarks of organic form is a sense of natural evolvement from one thing to the next. Nowhere is this more apparent than in the way one movement grows into another. This matter of transition is an important aspect of creating choreography that flows with its own inner kinesthetic logic; it is also a difficult choreographic concept to master.

There are transitions between individual movements, between phrases, and between major sections of a dance. The size and complexity of a transition is usually determined by the size and nature of what is connected. The most efficient transition between two movements should be as automatic and fluid as a plié between jumps and is usually determined by physical necessity. A transition between movement *phrases* can be tiny as a step, simple as a change of direction or focus, or it may be a movement phrase itself. Transitions between major sections are determined by the overall form or dramatic necessity. A transition should be only as long as it needs to be to fulfill its function; if it gets too long or takes on too much interest it ceases to be a transition.

No matter what the length or complexity, transitions must be an integral part of the dance. This of course does not mean they cannot be varied or vital. There are infinite ways of handling transitions, and what is right in one context is not necessarily appropriate somewhere else. Transitions can be gradual or abrupt; they can be achieved by simultaneously overlapping all or part of one movement with another; they can be efficient or cumbersome, simple or complex, obvious or subtle.

The following improv emphasizes how transitions can and do take place naturally, as if of their own accord.

Improv: The Turn-Around Place

Preparation: Walk backward, rather slowly, establishing a feeling of going in that direction, then, paying attention to the turn-around place, start walking forward.

The leader calls out a series of simple changes (e.g., changes of direction or level, an undulatory movement followed by a burst, the recovery from a plié, going from slow motion into sudden jolts), making sure that the changes include ones of time and force, rhythm or movement quality, as well as space. The dancers respond accordingly, simply paying attention to the turn-around place, observing the natural transition that occurs. Attention may be called to any element, such as what happens to the breathing, or to whether the change took place abruptly or gradually, or if other parts of the body came into play. The dancers then experiment with the same change ideas but with a different movement—again, initially just observing what occurs. Awareness is focused on that indeterminate instant when up becomes down, in becomes out, soft turns into hard. Then, working with the indicated change, the dancer explores a variety of ways of accomplishing that particular turnaround. When this process of (1) simply doing the change called for, (2) observing it, (3) actively experimenting with many different responses to it, is completed, the leader gives another change idea and the sequence is repeated.

Short & to the Point: Overlapping Transition
Set two short movement phrases, one with the hands and the other with the feet. Perform them starting one before you finish the other.

Choreographic Study/Improv: Familiar Links
Set a series of five very short movement phrases that can work within one dance. Perform them with transitions, making the transitions distinctly different from the five phrases yet not jarring, so that they also fit in the same dance. Unite all the transitions in some way, for example, with the same movement quality (shaking), with the same motif (opening and closing of the fist), with the same kind of movement (turning).

Choreographic Study/Improv: Growing a Monster
Set two short movement phrases. Start with a very short transition from the first to the second. Each time you repeat phrase-transition-phrase increase the length of the transition—one second, three seconds, five seconds. . . . At what point does it cease to be a transition?

Discuss the danger of the transition outweighing or obscuring the main movement themes.

Perform the phrase-transition-phrase again. As you increase the length of the transition let it take over and become the main movement, while the original movement fades and becomes secondary or transitional.

Choreographic Studies: A Variety of Transitions
Set two short movement phrases, the first of which ends in a *significantly different place, physically,* from where the second

begins (e.g., phrase A is a turn-fall, while phrase B begins with a one-legged relevé balance). Create four different transitions, as indicated below, to connect the two phrases.

1. Find the most efficient link between the two. What is physically necessary to get from the end of A to the beginning of B? What are some of the ways that it could be accomplished: a stretch, a series of stillnesses, etc.

2. Create a complicated, obtuse, and very obvious way to effect the transition, perhaps even cumbersome. This is a good place to exploit humorous or comic possibilities.

3. Stretch the end of A into space or time so that it propels itself into B and becomes an impulse or initiating agent for the second phrase.

4. Use the material from both A and B to make the transition, thus letting the transition be absorbed into the flow of the two phrases.

Sequencing

A dance isn't sewn together hit or miss like a crazy quilt, and the phrase so often used, "building a dance," is not as offhand a remark as it may at first seem. Careful attention must be paid to organization all along the way, as the dance grows from single movements to short and long phrases, to sequences and sections, on its way to becoming a completed piece. The choreographer has to arrive at what, for her, is a sensible ordering of all those bits and phrases.

Having already dealt with small phrases (see chapter 4) and transitions as basic elements in building dances, let's now turn our attention to the next stage—that of putting the movements and phrases together into larger units. Regardless of the size of the pieces we're working with, we must ask ourselves some basic questions: What is the order that is most expressive of the choreographic intent? What provides the best transitions, either aesthetically or physically? Which order gives the smaller units, when joined together, a unified and total shape as a larger whole? (This is directly related to the building of climaxes and overall form.) Sometimes the order suggests itself. Sometimes it takes a little experimenting and rearranging until the right sequence is found.

Choreographic Study: Arrange and Rearrange
Create three short movement phrases and teach them to someone else. These phrases are then shown strung together in all possible combinations (1–2–3, 3–2–1, 2–1–3, 2–3–1, 1–3–2, and 3–1–2) while the creator of the phrases (and others in the group) watch. Discuss how changes in sequence change and affect the meaning, the phrasing, the overall form or climax, the sense of beginning-middle-end.

There are times when chance is used to decide sequence and other choreographic aspects of a dance; it becomes part of the form, intent, and results. We deal with this as a choreographic device later in this chapter.

As we combine phrases we form larger units, not just a string of smaller ones, but *sequences* with a form of their own. The phrase-sentence analogy can be extended here to sequence-paragraph. They also have a beginning-middle-end, go somewhere, and are about some one thing, as is true of any phrase. They are made up of a number of phrases and have a climax or high point. The length and shapes of phrases and sequences vary according to the needs of the movement, image, and individual interpretation. Some possibilities are shown in figure 3.

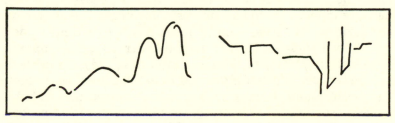

Figure 3

Exploratory Work

Play graphically with various combinations of phrase shapes and lengths to make a sequence. Draw several.

Improv: Dance-a-Graph

Pick your favorite drawing and improvise on it. (You can add an image and work with that as stimulus if you want.) Remember: beginning-middle-end, all about one thing, a high point. Try a different drawing.

Compositional Structures vs. Choreographic Devices

We are now ready to deal with two fundamental entities of choreography, compositional structures and choreographic devices. An important thing to realize first of all is that these two categories operate independently of one another. They do not exist in any set order of priority. The choreographer, in actual practice, may attend to either of them first. More than likely, there will be times when one necessarily takes precedence over the other in the development of a given work. There will be other times when they progress and are dealt with rather simultaneously, even though they are each unique and do not overlap in their functions.

Choreographic devices are ways of developing nuggets of movement, thereby enriching and extending an initial movement in order to build a greater body of choreographic material. The original material is manipulated and amplified to yield more from a little; to enrich what is pedestrian, mundane, or mimetic; or to add interest, breadth, and depth. They are devices, not tricks, used by many artists in various fields.

Compositional structures, on the other hand, are frameworks or structures, as the label indicates. They are models having sequential patterns gleaned from the natural world that have been found to work well artistically. Even though they are set, if approached creatively they can produce various organic realizations. The choreographic material (developed and enriched via choreographic devices) may then be shaped into any of these structures.

So choreographic devices are ways for developing and filling out movement seeds, while compositional structures are classical frameworks used to determine the overall structure of an entire dance piece (or a substantial section thereof). Some of the compositional structures that we used are based on formal structures found in music and others are gleaned from art and literature.

Compositional Structures

AB Form

One of the simplest forms is AB: a theme and a contrasting theme. In a simple framework, this form provides one way of attaining the contrast and variety which is elemental in life and essential in a composed work (see pp. 108–10 for discussion of Unity-Variety-Contrast). The concept of unity is equally important, so it becomes necessary for A and B to have some common element. To provide this unity, we'll explore contrast as two sides of the same coin. A and B share a common arena, but from opposing or contradicting perspectives. The going from A to B requires some sort of transition to provide the connecting link, the bridge.

Exploratory Work: AB Form
Write a long list of pairs of words that are opposites. Star all the ones that could lend themselves easily to movement.

Improv: Opposites
Pick a pair of words from your list. Improvise on one of them (e.g., fast of fast/slow). Really get into that word-idea; actually try to embody and become it. Keep repeating the word you've chosen to work with to yourself. Feel it become a part of you and you a part of it. Try to move with the essence of that word. Experiment with different movements that home in on it. Be-

come aware of a movement that you're doing that seems to best epitomize that word. Repeat that movement several times, getting a good feel for it, so you will know it well. Do the same with another movement that captures the essence of the same word; repeat it. Put a few of these movements together so they work as a unit. (The phrase or sequence you've just done is A.) Gradually feel the word-idea diminish in importance and hear the voice of its opposite. Begin working with the opposite word-idea in the same way. Once again, work at it until you come up with an improvisational sequence for B. You now have two loosely set sequences, A and B.

To put the two together (thereby producing an AB form), you'll have to pay attention to the transition between them. One possibility is to change abruptly from one to the other; another is to do a series of abrupt back-and-forth changes, as with a contest or tease between the two; or the transition may take the form of a gradual shift from A to B along the AB continuum.

Choreographic Study: AB Form
Using the A and B sequences developed in the preceding improv, and determining the nature of the transition you want to employ, create a dance study in AB form. Keep the transition brief.

ABA Form

An extension of the AB form is ABA, and a modified version of that is ABA'. Using the material in the previous assignment, let's go through the process of creating an ABA' sequence. Take A and shorten it, condensing and using only its salient features. One way to condense is to do simultaneously two movements that were previously done separately (a thematic arm gesture coupled with a thematic walking pattern). There should be no repetition of any movements, for within so short a study, the original theme needs to have a maximum of content with a minimum of internal manipulations. This new, shortened phrase is A'.

Choreographic Study: ABA'
Now work out a transition from B to A'. Show the resulting study: A-transition-B-transition-A'.

Rondo

A further extension of the AB form is the rondo, ABACADA (sounds like abracadabra!). Rondo has a basic theme A that keeps returning in a pure or modified form, A or A', after related but contrasting themes are explored. In any given work you can repeat A or, after starting A as the original theme, you can repeat it as A'. This is the familiar form of ballads, in which there are verses with a repeated refrain.

Improv: Rondo
Begin moving in a small contained space with nervous energy. This will be your A theme. Using images if you want to, experiment with contrasting material for B, C, D, returning to A between each exploration. You may want to have A always in the same place in the room. ♦ Begin . . .

Natural Forms

Some of the progressions occurring in nature can be utilized by the choreographer for both subject matter and overall form. These include life cycles (a butterfly or tree), universal patterns (day/night, the seasons, evolution), and behavioral patterns (hunting-cooking-eating). The transformation of these natural images into works of art may require forms unique to one artist's perception or that of a commonly used pattern (day/night = AB). In either case, the forms are organic in origin. Humphrey's *Day on Earth* is a beautiful example of a choreographic realization of the life cycle of a family in which a natural form served as the subject matter for a dance.

Improv: Life Cycle
For each stage of a human's life cycle (child, youth, adult, old age) choose a descriptive movement word and improvise to it. ϙ Begin . . .

Choreographic Study: Life Cycle
Create a study using the material from the above improv. Pay attention to the transitions and how the ending relates to the beginning.
   Discussion. Is your translation of the life cycle different from that shown by others? The terms you choose will reflect your feelings about each age; consequently, the substance of the dances shown will differ (e.g., whether you see an infant as primarily helpless or inquisitive).

Choreographic Study: Natural Progressions
Make a list of universal patterns (or progressions) and of behavioral patterns. Then, using one of the images, create a study, letting the image serve both as subject matter and as form.

Narrative

Everyone loves a good story, witness the popularity of minstrels, the Bible, *The Arabian Nights*. Stories come in all forms: fables, myths, allegories, anecdotes. Both modern dance and ballet use stories for content and structure.

Although the standard plots are used over and over again, they never lose their popularity. Lost child has fantastic adventure and safely returns home. Boy meets girl—boy loses girl—boy wins her back. Villain intimidates innocents—hero to the rescue. The individual storyteller (writer, choreographer, or lyricist) imaginatively colors in the specifics of character, location, and style, making use of action and surprise.

When you add the possibilities of flashbacks and daydreaming, the narrative form allows the use of material that would not necessarily fit a straight real-time story. Because dance is nonliteral, it easily accommodates complex juxtaposing of fantasies, memories, nightmares, and present events. Bringing these together allows for psychological overtones, insights. Graham sometimes takes advantage of this by focusing on one character and showing what is going on in her head. A dialogue between past and present is possible.

> *Improv: Narrative*
> ◊ Once upon a time you set off from home to see the world—young, enthusiastic, confident . . . soon you become involved in the fast pace and crowded space of city life . . . over the years the tensions begin to tell . . . you return home in old age to rest.

People's favorite stories are about themselves. Short tales, complete or partial autobiographies, frustrated dreams or miraculous fantasies—each provides wonderful source material.

> *Choreographic Study: Autobiography*
> Create a partial autobiographical study. It can be as simple in form as the life cycle or it can contain complexities as suggested above.

Collage

A collage is a work of art consisting of bits and pieces of assorted materials that are brought together to create a whole. Their juxtaposition, simultaneously apprehended, creates a unified effect, which can be surrealistic, incongruous, or absurd. When successful, the immediate interplay of the diverse ingredients does not appear hodge-podge, but shows new relationships, creating a different or stronger statement than would be possible if only one kind of material was used.

Collage is a compositional structure that has been primarily pursued in the visual (and therefore timeless) arts, since it requires the simultaneity of diverse aspects. Dance is temporal, so in order for the collage effect to work, the juxtaposing must occur through the overlapping or close succession of movements. A series of different lengthy themes (A,B,C,D,) would not fulfill the requirements of a collage, whereas bits and pieces of contrasting momentary movements juxtaposed to create a unified effect would. It could be a pastiche of discordant events having a unified thread, or it could be an overlay of mediums in a more incongruous and tidbit way than is generally achieved through mixed media. (In mixed media, although the various modes do occur concurrently, they each usually work within their own idiom rather than constantly crossing over, shifting, weaving in, out, amongst, and betwixt one another.)

The simultaneous, incongruous juxtaposing necessary for collage is not to be confused with chance, which is what Merce Cunningham, John Cage, and Robert Rauschenberg used in their collaborations involving independent creations performed coincidentally. First, collage involves the scrambling of tiny bits and pieces, not large chunks, and second, it involves a conscious integration of focus, of a specific intent for the work.

Remember that although the collage has a specific focus, it is fragmentary, coincidental, and complex by nature, capable of eliciting varied and multiple responses. Just as the visual artist pursues the contents of his desk, garbage pail, and glove compartment for contributing material, you as a life artist must look as well to the whole range of ordinary/extraordinary movement behavior.

While a collage is not necessarily incongruous or illogical, the form certainly lends itself to those possibilities. It will support themes of insanity, dreams, chaos (a fact which led to its embrace by the Surrealists). While the content and resulting form may appear illogical, it is essential that the form work *as a whole*.

Exploratory Work

Look at collages in the visual arts, works by Surrealists. Bring in examples. Can you find an apparent focus or theme for each piece? Why or how does it fit into the category of collage? What possibilities, if any, for dance do you see in them?

Choreographic Study: Dance Collage
Consciously identify one finite, concrete thing that will serve
as your common thread. Collect and create many things apper-
taining to it. Create a study employing these in conjunction
with an open attitude toward movement.

Theme and Variation vs. Motif and Development

Even though theme and variation is a compositional structure, and motif and development is a choreographic device,
they are so often and easily confused that it's necessary to
make the distinction between them as clear as possible. The
basic difference between a theme and a motif is in how they
are used. Simply put, the theme is varied, while the motif is
developed—what could make more sense?

With a theme, the internal sequence remains constant. (This
is how theme and variation is understood and used in music.)
While each variation on the theme gives it a different character (or face), the basic order of the original is unaltered.
Once the original theme is presented, the sequence of variations can be changed around, that is, variation 3 could be
performed after variation 6 and followed by variation 2. The
form of theme and variation does not require that variation 2
follow variation 1. However, a given instance might require
that the variations do indeed progress in a certain sequence to
convey the intent of a specific piece: for example, a life
journey in which the variations show the different ways that a
child, a young woman, and a old woman would execute a
given theme.

The end result of a theme and variation is a sequence consisting of a movement phrase repeated a number of times with
different shadings. The end result of motif and development
can be any number of different movements or phrases developed organically by manipulating the motif. (Motif and development is explained on pp. 101–07). Compare the graphic il-

lustration for theme and variation with the one for motif and development (fig. 4).

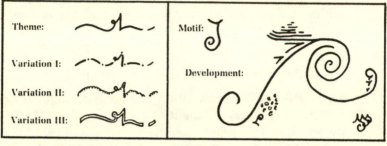

Figure 4

As you work through these two categories, the nature of their difference will become more apparent. Some discussion prior to and after improvising and composing in these categories will help to clarify your understanding even further.

Theme and Variation

A theme is a clear movement sequence that can be used as a basic structure for different variations. This movement sequence needs variety and interest in directions and level for any but the most sophisticated renderings. There should not be any repeats in the theme. Since you may have ten variations, you certainly do not want to see any one movement more than the ten times, no matter how exciting or varied it is.

Variations keep the same sequence of time and movement as in the original theme, but have their own character, color, flavor. You can name each variation, for example, a withering or aloof variation. One way to consider it is by having different types of people doing the same theme (sneaky thief, carefree three-year-old, sophisticated duchess, and so on).

The basic idea of Theme and Variation is treated somewhat differtly in painting, a timeless art, than in music or dance, which are temporal. Instead of following a given time sequence in which the order of occurrence in that sequence is inviolate, it is the spatial order that is adhered to. Monet's *Poplars* series depicts the same scene at different times of day, the variations being shown by the differing use of light. Theme and variation is found in folk dances—the Greek Pantozali has five strict and clear variations; while modern examples are often not very strict (e.g., Jerome Robbins's *Waltz*).

Exploratory Work
Make a list of possible movement variations (e.g., skippy, through the mud).

Improv: Variations on a Theme
Use a set theme, your own, or the one given here: Take four steps forward, starting on the right foot; step out to second position plié; tilt to the right; turn to the right.

Have everyone do the basic theme. Then repeat while improvising a "dragging" variation, a "shaky" variation. Now try the variations from your own list. Do not impose a time structure (or set tempo) on the variations. Divide the group in two. One group watches while the other improvises on their variations to the given theme. ◊

Choreographic Study: Theme and Variation
Compose a new theme and choreograph four variations.

Choreographic Devices

These have previously been explained as ways of developing and filling out movement seeds. The first of these is motif and development, which we have already differentiated from theme and variation (for review, see pp. 99–100).

Motif and Development

In motif and development, the motif itself is manipulated; it is performed upside down, backward, inside out. Its original sequence (the order of its parts) is not sacred as in theme and variation. Fragments of the movement are used and developed separately, then put together with no specific regard for the original sequential order. But there is a definite sense of form that comes from developing the motif. The form is often self-serving, unique to the particular development of that particular motif.

A motif is a single movement or a short movement phrase (usually shorter than a theme) that is used as a source or a spark for development into an integrated gestalt. The motif can contain the essence for the complete piece (see fig. 4). The best known example is Beethoven's Fifth Symphony where the entire piece is built on the development of the first four notes.

We have developed a schema of sixteen possible ways to manipulate a motif. Here are some things to keep in mind as you work through them. Try each manipulation on your movement motif. Take a tidbit of time (ten to twenty seconds) to improvise on each before going on to the next. As you go along, observe other people's solutions so that you can immediately see the range and wealth of development these can lead to, for virtually everyone comes up with some interesting interpretations. It turns into a game, inventive and mutually supportive. It is important to explore each of the sixteen ways in as pure a form as possible, without combining any two ways. For example, don't change the spatial range of the original movement as a by-product of doing it faster or slower. To begin, each person comes up with a single movement, a motif. For this initial exploration, it shouldn't end where it began. Keep it simple, for example, a three-quarter arm circle with a twist at the end; an open-closing-dropping of the fist; tracing a simple spatial pattern (⌒ , ↺) in the air with your hand.

Sixteen Ways to Manipulate a Motif

1. *Repetition.*   Repeat exactly the same.
2. *Retrograde.*   Perform it backward. Start at the end and follow it back through space—like a movie run backward.
3. *Inversion: upside-down* (⌒ becomes ⌄) or *lateral*

(⌢ becomes ⌣). For upside-down inversion, you may have to lie on the floor or stand on your head. (This can be tricky and often impossible, but don't dismiss it on those grounds.)

4. *Size: condense/expand.* Take the motif and do it as small as you can. Try it even smaller. Now take the movement and make it bigger, as big as you can.

5. *Tempo: fast/slow/stop.* Take the motif and do it as fast as possible. Try again, even faster. Be careful not to let it get smaller. Do it as slowly as you can. Remember to keep the space constant, the same size it was originally. Find places for stillness in it.

6. *Rhythm.* Vary the rhythm but not the tempo. The variety and pattern of the beats should be altered, not the speed or the length of time it takes to accomplish. If, for example, the original rhythm was ♩ ♩, try doing it ♫ ♩ ♩.

7. *Quality.* Vary the movement quality. Try the same movement quivery, drifting, with erratic tension, etc.

8. *Instrumentation.* Perform the movement with a different body part; try several different parts of the body. Let another performer do it. Have a whole group do it.

9. *Force.* Vary the amount of force you use in producing the movement. Do it with a great deal of strength, from beginning to end. Now repeat it again, with very little force, gently, weakly. Carefully try to keep the change in force only.

10 *Background.* Change the design of the rest of the body from its original position and repeat the motif. Let the rest of the body be doing something while the motif is going on. Sit instead of stand. Try perhaps twisting all the rest of you into a knot while still performing the regular motif. Add another person (maybe having them wrap around you). Add to or change the set, the lighting.

11. *Staging.* Perform it at a different place on the stage and/or with a different facing to the audience, sideways or on a diagnonal.

12. *Embellishment (ornamentation).* The movement itself

can have the embellishment (e.g., little loops or jigjags occurring along the path of the movement); or a part of the body can be embellished as it is involved in the movement (as the arm moves, wiggle the fingers or make a fist); or try embellishing both the body and the path of movement at the same time.

13. *Change of Planes/Levels.* Change the motif to a different plane: the horizontal, the vertical, the sagittal plane or any other slice of space. Do it on a different level. Trace the path of the gesture and use it as a floor pattern. Move along that.

14. *Additive/Incorporative.* Additive: While doing the original motif, simultaneously execute any kind of jump, turn, or locomotor pattern (triplet, run, slide). Incorporative: Make the original motif into a jump, turn, or locomotor pattern. Although this can be tough or impossible with some motifs, approach it with a sense of "how can x [original motif] be jumped, turned, moved from place to place?" A series of chassés would be an example of the way an arc could be realized as a locomotor pattern.

15. *Fragmentation.* Use only a part of the motif, any part. Use it as an entity in itself. Use it to attend to a detail, a part worth isolating that might otherwise be overlooked. Or use several parts of it, but not the whole thing—such as the beginning third, a tiny piece halfway through, and the very, very end.

16. *Combination.* Combine any of the above so that they happen at the same time. This lets you combine affinities (faster with smaller) or antagonists (faster with larger) for choreographic interest and technical challenge. Fragmentation is particularly effective when combined with others. You may combine three or four manipulations at the same time (fragmentation/inversion/embellishment, or inversion/retrograde/slower/different background). Variety and complexity grows as you combine more and more manipulations.

Play with combining several manipulations at the same time; it can be mental gymnastics, but fun. And don't settle for the first idea that comes to mind. For example, jump forward while doing an embellished version of the motif with a different part of the body as small as possible, landing with a quarter turn to a new facing in a lunge or on the floor while upside down.

Short & to the Point
Using your motif, perform the following as one phrase: original, slow-retrograde, quick-condensed, original.

Choreographic Study: Motif and Development
Create a new motif. Develop a study based on manipulating the motif. Every movement within your dance should be based on some kind of manipulation of that motif and you should be able to defend it on those grounds, specifically. Make it a complete dance, with considerations of phrasing, intention, stage placement, etc. Somewhere in the piece the original motif, *in its pure form*, must be executed.

Discussion. How well does the dance hold together when it is built from a motif? Does it feel as if everything comes from the same place, is related, and belongs in the same piece? Try to identify the original motif in the pieces shown.

In doing this study, stress the purity factor. We've found it particularly useful to be quite strict, insisting that every movement be substantiated via one or more of the sixteen ways. When you come up against a block (one of the sixteen ways that is impossible to apply to your motif), take a moment and have everyone try and find a solution, for it is the experience of experimentation, of poking into new territory, that still (and always) remains the primary aim. In its practical application, of course, motif and development is simply a tool in the craft of choreography. The manipulations are completely flexible, and the resulting movements become easily combined with other movements. The rules are bent or ignored in the service of the creative choreographic act.

Manipulating the motif in these various ways produces a lot

of material. The material is then combined to make larger and larger sequences. In this way, motif and development becomes amplified as it is applied to longer movement phrases, sequences, and whole sections. You work with the same sixteen principles in the same way but on a much bigger and more complex scale. Once you feel comfortable with the simpler movement version, try this:

Additional Work for an Extended Motif
Take a movement sequence (one that covers a fair amount of floor space) from something you've choreographed or from technique class and perform it as originally done. Then work it out in a space one-fourth the size; in a huge space (a gym or outside); in a long narrow hall. [This is great preparation for touring a piece, when performance areas vary so much.] Try it in retrograde. Choose other manipulations and do them. Now do a manipulation combining several ways.

When a dance or study evolves, it ideally incorporates the concept of unity-variety-contrast (see p. 108). The motif-and-development approach achieves this organically. There's unity in that it all came from the same motif; variety stemming from the different ways the motif was manipulated; and contrast occurring when two opposing ends of the continuum of a given manipulation (forward/retrograde, big/small) are used, or when two separate and independent motifs (and their assorted manipulations) are combined in a single dance.

It's useful to realize that motif and development is (at least in the initial stages of learning) a rather rote, cerebral approach to developing movement material. It is priceless for those days or moments when you find yourself in the studio and nothing is happening—when you're in a creative desert. Never again will the aspiring choreographer have to stand there, staring at the mirror and walls, waiting for divine inspiration to strike! As you become more and more competent, this approach will become second nature. No longer will you have to go down the list, manipulating that original motif according to specific suggestions, this way and that. You'll be able to do it spontaneously, unconsciously.

Improv: Motif and Development at an Advanced Level
Now that you have physically and intellectually experienced the possibilities of developing a motif, try doing it in an improvisational setting without analyzing as you go along. ◊ Pick a clear motif and improvise to it, allowing development to occur spontaneously. As you work, keep your feelers out—if an unrelated movement sneaks in, pass through it and go back to the original motif material.

If the device of motif and development has become part of the way you work, the foregoing should emerge as an organically varied and well-integrated improv.

Highlighting

Certain instants (movements or events) stand out more than others. They make an impact when they occur; they reverberate and remain with us as memories, images. Repeatedly, the choreographer will find himself wanting to highlight a particular moment, to set it apart. He singles it out and accentuates it, underlines it in some way, thus making it more salient. The choreographer may employ any of the space, time, energy elements in order to accomplish this, but its effect is that of hallowing an instant (or a moment or event) and, in this way, removing it from its ordinary place. (See pp. 63–65 for accent as specifically achieved through, and related to, the element of time.)

A movement can be highlighted by adding to, changing, or contrasting it. A movement that is substantially or unexpectedly longer or shorter, stronger or weaker, sparser or fuller than all the rest is different and thereby emphasized.

Exploratory Work
List ways of emphasizing movement, of highlighting an instant. Consider a variety of approaches, but be specific. In-

clude both the obvious and the subtle (e.g., a moment of weakness amidst a frantic barrage).

Short & to the Point
Create a phrase of eight to sixteen counts. Find the movement within it that you want to highlight. Then find another movement within the phrase and highlight that; another.

Improv: To the Glory of Sharmal
Since the obvious would be to have soft, gentle movement with the highlights being stronger, let's try the opposite: work with weaker, sparser, shorter as the highlights. ◊ You are a young enthusiastic disciple giving a sermon to the glory of the god Sharmal, who stands for meekness, smallness, tenderness. There is a large discrepancy between your enthusiastic, theatrical, histrionic, preaching style and the qualities of the god you are describing and serving.

Choreographic Study: Highlighting
Choreograph a study highlighting a variety of movements or utilizing various ways of highlighting one movement. Be careful not to have so much highlighting that it takes over and becomes the dominant content.

It's important to note that musical accents and choreographic highlights are but two of the contributing factors that help build to and create a climax. Accenting a beat or highlighting a movement enhances it so it is more visible, stands out from the surrounding material. It is a short-term occurrence. Climax, on the other hand, has a longer lifespan; it is the end of a developmental progression, an inevitable result of the direction of an entire dance or significant section thereof. (See p. 121 for further discussion of climax.)

Unity-Variety-Contrast

Although not actually a device, unity-variety-contrast functions integrally in the process of forming. A work of art is about "something"; that "something" is its unifying element.

The stuff of which it is made shares some common bond. The unity is the core that binds together the parts. As Alma Hawkins so elegantly states when speaking about unity, "It unfolds with a directness that seems to penetrate all superficiality and moves to the heart of the idea."[3] This should surely act as an underlying principle for choreographers.

Within the unity, we need variety. Variety is about adding breadth and developing different facets of the material. In motif and development, we dealt with creating variety by using manipulation. But providing variety within the context of unity is a concept essential to every aspect of the choreographic process dealt with in this book.

Contrast, the third part of the triumvirate, could be included within variety, for certainly an idea or development contrasting to the central one varies it in a fundamental way. But because contrast implies a specialized type of variety, it seems helpful to single it out. Contrast connotes a radically different point of view or manipulation, a substantial difference in perspective, the possibility for a clear and decided break; variety includes the slightest of dissimilarities. In dance, contrast occurs within a range, from instances having small significance (going from a frenzy to a freeze) to situations of great choreographic import (such as the dramatic confrontation in *Nutcracker* between the forces of good and the forces of evil, as personified by the Nutcracker and the Mouse King).

The artist is often singularly noted for this intuitive ability to juxtapose, match, or marry the totally incongruous in a way that fits or inexplicably relates. This use of contrast is often what produces the new awareness in a work of art. But no matter how far-ranging the discrepancies of variety and contrast, they all exist within the context of the unified theme of the dance.

Improv: Three Punches

φ Think about punching way out into space. Punch. Your punches have a *follow-through* and send echos way into the distance. Use all the parts of your body to accommodate all directions. Suddenly your punches are *stopped short* as if you hit an invisible brick wall. Keep punching with different parts of your body. Now the wall changes to rubber and your punches *rebound;* enjoy the rebound; play with how it affects your whole body. Randomly mix the three kinds of punches remembering to use elbows, chin, heel, buttocks, etc., to initiate the punch.

In pairs, one person is the puncher, the other is the responder. The puncher is the initiator and uses a variety of punches directed at his partner. The responder reacts in a valid way to the character of each of the punches. The distance between you may range from as close as is safe to as far as the punch is sensed. Change roles. Mix roles at random.

Discuss how the responder provided the contrast while still keeping the unity. How was the element of variety achieved within the unity? Remember, *unity* is the common bond that ties it all together; *variety* includes different facets of a given theme, coloration, gradation; while *contrast* can refer to opposites (as with a conflicting view) or to alternatives that are substantially different. Pay attention to the commonality between the different qualities you've chosen to work with.

Choreographic Study: Unity-Variety-Contrast
Using two or three movements or movement qualities that have some common aspect (e.g., push/pull, drop/climb, scatter/collect), create a study that will have unity-variety-contrast.

Minimal Movement

It is tempting to produce movement upon interesting movement, to explore and incorporate the body and all its parts when creating, getting them all actively involved. But just as the complex can obscure the simple, and the overt obliterate the subtle, so large movement can override small. We have shown the choreographic potential that stillness and subtely possess. Minimal movement, an often ignored device, is the use of a small and isolated movement or part of the body that takes on primary significance in the dance. Consideration must be given to the design of the rest of the body, since it serves as background (see pp. 43–45). All is still, save that single voice, speaking in a quiet tone that demands full concentration. And if it is the only thing going on onstage, it forces the audience to strain their eyes to hear it:

an errant twitching that alights on one part of the body
barely visible rocking (as with intense grief)
a shiver
a whole section choreographed for fingers and palm of the left hand.

Choreographic Study: The Smallest Voice
Think of something very small but very important that you want to say or show. Create a context for it that involves several other dancers. Maximize this opportunity to use minimal movement.

Canon

Canon is one of the most satisfying forms because it has unity and variety built right into it. Basically, it is a single theme executed at different times. It is particularly satisfying in dance because it
re-creates the lost moment
       re-creates the lost moment
              re-creates the lost moment. Dance, after all, is a series, a continuous progression of lost moments.
    In a strict sense, especially in music, canon is considered a formal compositional structure. We have chosen to regard it as a choreographic device because rarely is an entire dance (or lengthy section within a dance) canonized strictly and exclusively for purposes of achieving a structure or overall form. It is used rather as a device for achieving breadth and increasing complexity.
    Although "Row, Row, Row, Your Boat" is probably the most familiar canon of all, it represents only one of several forms that a canon can take. First we'll work within the category of

strict canons, which includes reverting (overlapping and non-overlapping), simultaneous, and cumulative. In these, a limited number of movements recur exactly the same at different times. Then we'll deal with loose canon, which provides a freer way to employ the canon device.

```
I. Strict
   A. Reverting
      1. Overlapping
      2. Nonoverlapping
   B. Simultaneous
   C. Cumulative
II. Loose
```

In a reverting canon, each person does the entire phrase, from beginning to end, starting at periodic intervals. Each entry reverts to the beginning, producing a delayed time effect. The movement may or may not overlap.

Reverting—overlapping	Reverting—nonoverlapping
Dancer A: 1 2 3	Dancer A: 1 2 3
Dancer B: 1 2 3	Dancer B: 1 2 3
Dancer C: 1 2 3	Dancer C: 1 2 3

Note: Because the improvisations for canon are more sophisticated, we suggest that you precede them by the Mirroring or Second Skin Shadowing improvisations (pp. 20, 56).

Improv: Echo

Work in pairs. One person is the voice, the other person is the echo. The voice speaks (does a simple movement phrase) and freezes. The second dancer then exactly echoes (repeats) that movement. The first dancer speaks again and freezes again. At all times, only one of the two dancers is moving—when the speaker is frozen, the echo is echoing; when the echo has completed its echo, the speaker immediately moves again. After a while, change roles.

It will soon become apparent that this improv is easier to do if certain conditions are met: (1) the movement phrase must be kept fairly short and simple; (2) the movement must be done within sight lines so that the echoer is not left looking away from the speaker, for then she couldn't "hear" the next phrase; (3) whereas the Mirroring or Shadowing improvs necessitated slower motion, without any sudden starts or stops, the Echo allows for quick movement and abrupt changes. It is, in fact, easier for the echoer to remember and repeat a phrase having a broader spectrum and greater diversity in its use of space, time, and energy.

In the Echo improv, we've been creating the kind of canon in which the dancers do not overlap each other's movement:

```
              Reverting—nonoverlapping
Dancer A:  1  2  3  4           5  6  7  8
Dancer B:           1  2  3  4           5  6  7  8
```

If you were to overlap the phrases, the time line would look like this:

```
              Reverting—overlapping
Dancer A:  1  2  3  4  5  6  7  8
Dancer B:        1  2  3  4  5  6  7  8
```

Or the overlap could be greater:

```
              Reverting—overlapping
Dancer A:  1  2  3  4  5  6  7  8
Dancer B:     1  2  3  4  5  6  7  8
```

The next two improvs, are also reverting canons, but they employ overlapping, whereas the Echo improv did not.

Improv: Reverting—Overlapping Canon (visual)
Again, everyone works in pairs, with one person as originator, one as follower. It is helpful to have some members accompany while others participate. The accompanists will set a moderate

tempo. The originator improvises to the beat in units of four-count phrases. The follower stays four counts behind. It is the follower's task to do movement phrase A (the first four counts) while watching (and capturing, learning, remembering) movement phrase B (the next four counts). The emphasis and attention must be on clarity of movement, accuracy of timing. Here again, more experienced dancers will probably be able to handle more complex rhythmic patterns, so instead of four quarter-note movements, they can work with ♩♫♩ or ♩♪♪♫♫ . Or they could extend the phrase to eight counts and increase the challenge! Switch roles.

Improv: Reverting—Overlapping Canon (aural)

If you are fortunate enough to have a good accompanist (on piano, guitar, flute, whatever) have her improvise a continuous stream of music in 4/4 time, changing the rhythmic pattern in each measure. Then all the dancers simultaneously move to the rhythm, one measure later. Each dancer will do his own movement. This is a slightly different problem from the first version because it necessitates and trains aural rather than visual recall, as well as reinterpretation from one medium to another.

If a musician is not available, get into pairs and let one be the accompanist and one the dancer; then, with simple sounds or vocalizations, the musician of each pair furnishes the sound score to be repeated in movement by the dancer. Either case (one accompanist for the whole class or paired accompanist/dancer) allows for changes between measures and in accent, tempo, meter, dynamics, etc.

Both the aural and visual versions of the reverting canon are useful to the dancer and should be attempted and worked with. You may find the aural canon actually easier to do than the visual one. It is best to keep the length of phrase in a visual (or movement) canon the same each time until the dancers have become adept at this exercise. For a further challenge, combine the visual and the aural canons.

Short & to the Point: Intrabody Canon

Using different parts of your body as the various voices, try a reverting canon. Keep the material simple initially. Was it the overlapping version? If not, try that one, too.

While the ability to do the canon is a good skill to have, the point is to see and understand all the aspects of the canon at work. Therefore it would be good to have half the group watch while the others improvise. Seeing the different effects is as important as doing them.

As mentioned before, the simultaneous and the cumulative canons (like the reverting canon) are categorically strict forms.

In a simultaneous canon, all participants do the same phrase at the same time, but have different starting points:

	Simultaneous			
Dancer A:	1	2	3	4
Dancer B:	2	3	4	1
Dancer C:	3	4	1	2
Dancer D:	4	1	2	3

The cumulative canon is a series of staggered entries: each person joins in with the movement in progress, but all end at the same time. This form of canon is cumulative in effect. The first person does the entire phrase. The second person starts later, joining in to do the same thing that the first is doing *at the time she joins her.*

	Cumulative			
Dancer A:	1	2	3	4
Dancer B:		2	3	4
Dancer C:			3	4
Dancer D:				4

A more flexible version of this would be:

Dancer A:	1	2	3	4	5
Dancer B:		2		4	5
Dancer C:			3	4	5
Dancer D:					5

Choreographic Study: Strict Canon
Teach the entire class a phrase using four or five movements.
Form three groups—one each for reverting, simultaneous, cumulative. Each group arranges and shows its version of the
movement phrase as a canon.

In a loose canon (as the name indicates) one can take more
freedoms. Remember a canon consists of one phrase that is
executed at different times by at least two different voices in
an overlapping or sequential relationship. (1) You could
change the spatial relationship—facing, level, direction, location on stage. (2) You could incorporate freezes or extraneous
material, improvised on the spot or preset, woven in and out.
(3) You could keep the sequence and timing constant, but vary
the amount or nature of the force used.

Choreographic Study: Loose Canon
In groups of four or five, jointly create a study based on loose
canon.

Exploratory Work
Make a list of possible images that could utilize any of the
canon effects: "The Haunted Mirror," "The Past Repeats," "Oh,
no—not again!"

*Choreographic Study: Canonononing (or How Long
Can a Canon Canon On?)*
In groups of three or four create a repeatable phrase of four
movements such that you can make the transition from the last
movement back to the first without any additional movement.
Include at least one traveling sequence within the phrase. Create a short dance using only (or primarily) the repeatable
phrase, employing at least three kinds of canon as discussed in
this section: the strict forms of reverting (overlapping or nonoverlapping), simultaneous, and cumulative, and the loose
form. Be careful not to let the different canon forms make it
confusing or cluttered. The whole thing has to work together.
Discuss.

Chance

Chance is another device that can be used in choreograph-ing. It is a process whereby the choreographer decides to give up his own self will and, to some extent, leave decisions in the hands of fate or of his dancers. One can use it to produce both content and order.

Composer John Cage has pioneered the use of chance as a formulative device in art. He has collaborated for many years with Merce Cunningham, the first well-known choreographer to apply this approach to the field of dance. And apply it he has, in all ways, modes, and manners, as it has continued to intrigue and delight him. The notion of the coincidence of events, in time and space, is one of the things that this approach allows for. "Cunningham uses chance much as he might a magnet, to draw possibilities to him from beyond his reach and to arrange his materials . . . into relationships he might not otherwise have seen."[4]

But chance as a device has other uses. The saying "the die is cast" can be interpreted in two ways to show how chance can intervene in and affect the creative process.

In the first way, the die is "precast," that is, chance is used during the formative stages of creating the dance. Some arbitrary mechanism such as dice, coins, or the *I Ching* determines any aspect of the dance that the choreographer wishes to leave to the gods—content, sequence, form, the relation between the dancers, whatever. In this way the dance is decided by chance, worked out by the choreographer or dancer, and set. From then on, it does not change.

In the second way, the die is cast during the dance itself; the chance element is in operation while the performance is taking place. *Indeterminacy* is a term sometimes applied to this method of using chance. This approach leaves many decisions up to the discretion of the individual performers, including the dancers, the musicians, the lighting crew, and others. Prior to performance, the dancers may be given a certain number of movements or dance phrases. Each dancer then has as many options open to her as the choreographer allows in terms of how, when, and where she will use that material. The range of possibilities could include, for example, any of the motif and development manipulation done at whim; making on-the-spot decisions concerning which of the given movements she will do, in what order, with how many repetitions; when she chooses to enter or exit; where she will be onstage; who she will join, oppose, or interact with, and so forth. In other words, the dice are rolled as the dance is rolled,; as it gets danced, it takes on its own shape, content, and form. The dance is different each time it is performed.

Improv: A Chancy Dance for Six (two versions)
The first version uses chance to preset the dance, while the second uses chance during the performance of the dance. Both versions should be done since they are used in relationship to one another when performed and discussed.

Version I. You'll be rolling dice to determine the movements and choreograph a dance for six dancers.

Part A. First, assign each number on a die to a different part of the body (including one number for the whole body). Then do the same for six movement qualities, six locomotor movements (including stationary), six uses of time, and six uses of space. You'll have to roll the die five times (since there are five categories) to determine *each* of the six basic movements that will comprise the contents of the dance (thirty rolls in all with each movement being comprised of five rolls: a body part, a movement quality, a time component, space component, and a locomotor pattern). Make a list to keep track of these. Then improvise, devising movements that combine the elements that the roll of the die has determined (e.g., "the elbow glides while you quickly walk a circular path" would be one movement).

Part B. Assign each dancer a number (or let a roll of the die determine that as well). Then throw the die to find which movements she'll be doing, how many times each will be repeated, where it will be executed (having previously assigned a number to each of six stage areas and to each of six different possible facings). Assign each movement a number and throw again to determine the order in which the movements will occur, etc. Having used the die to set the content and order (what will happen when), rehearse. Although the process sounds complex, it will actually produce a dance that's just a few minutes long.

Version II. Using only the six movements derived in part A of version I, each dancer determines all the aspects in part B *as she performs.* In this way, the chance element is in operation during the actual performance.

Show version I and version II immediately following one another. Then compare and contrast the dances produced by the two different methods. They will have similar content. Talk about them from both the spectators' and the dancers' points of view.

Noa Eschald in Israel does her choreography by computer, in the notation system that the computer uses. This is one instance of the die being "precast" and exemplifies yet another approach.

Scoring is another chance device. A score for a dance is like the rules for a game; the dancer reads, interprets, and responds to it. When a choreographer creates a score, he determines the symbols, what (if anything) they represent, how and by whom they will be read.[5] One of Trish Brown's favorites is using the walls (inside or outside) of any building or room as the score to be read and responded to in movement.

Exploratory Work
Collect a series of interesting pictures, photographs.

Improv: Picture Score
Use the pictures as your score. Dance your interpretation.

Graphics are most often used. A key is established which equates a graphic mark (color, shape) with a given response (jump, burst of song). You can create a structure in which one dancer's response becomes another's cue. Scores can determine anything from the movement, to sound accompaniment, to interplay between the dancers, to use of props and clothing, to imitating the spectators. They can be strict or allow for a wide range of interpretation. The possibilities are endless.

Choreographic Study: Score-a-Dance
Create a visual dance score for a group of flexible size. Show and explain it. Then stage it, using the available people.

Improv-Study: By Breckenridge Lardé (done as a group)
Choose a word or theme (fighting, verticality, softness, etc.). Have everyone write down on three separate bits of paper three short phrases that the word brings to mind. Collect the papers, mix them up, and put them in random order. The result will be a group-created poem. Read the poem aloud. Have each person take three successive lines of the poem and create a brief dance phrase from them (verbalizing the lines along with the movement). This can be as literal or abstract a movement interpretation as the individual desires. Show your phrases to one another. Do them sequentially with each dancer moving only during her part and remaining frozen the rest of the time, or if you'd like, learn each other's sequences, string them together, and do the entire dance as one group. Dance-voice the resulting dance-poem.

We have dealt with six major choreographic devices: (motif and development, highlighting, unity-variety-contrast, minimal movement, canon, chance). If you are familiar with Effort/Shape theory and terminology as a qualitative and attitudinal way of dealing with movement, its concepts provide another choreographic device for enriching, modifying, and expanding choreographic and movement material. We'll now step back and view the piece from a larger perspective.

Overall Form

Whatever the form, and no matter how complex, the piece must work as a unit. The overall form includes how a dance builds, peaks, and concludes. The flow of the piece, how it picks up and rolls along, can be thought of as its *time line*. The nature of the time line in a particular dance is achieved both by the type of the individual movements and by how they evolve from one to another and feed off each other.

Sometimes entire dances move quickly (a hot jazz number), while others are slow. The same is true of sections within dances. For instance, the second act of *La Bayadère* begins with a mesmerizing, repetitive arabesque sequence performed by the corps as they enter in a long, snaking line. The time line may be thought of as analogous to driving: one could have the stop-go of city traffic, the all-out speed of the Indy 500, the ease and flow of a Sunday drive in the country.

Pacing is the process of building the dance layer upon layer, inviting the audience along every step of the way. When you have a twenty-minute dance, you need to pace it so you don't finish it in the first five minutes. A dance that is well-paced leads from the first movement directly to the last, even if it takes twenty minutes (or sixty, or ninety) to do so. To achieve this, you tease, connive, invite, take pertinent side roads, introduce intrigues, develop nuances. But it is all to the point, within the direct line of that dance's development.

A *climax* is the accumulated high point of the piece, consciously prepared for and built toward. It has a history, a reason for being where and how it is. Usually it is the result of a crescendo and often has a resolution. In a longer piece there is often a secondary climax which can help gather momentum and serve as a push toward the main climax. It may be a foreshadowing of the main one or could serve as a contradiction or commentary. In any case, the various sections and climaxes evolve from one to another and serve in the cumulative pacing of a piece.

The pacing and climax contribute to the dance's evolution and final movements. "Don't leave the ending till the end," says Doris Humphrey, you must prepare for it and you must prepare your audience for it.[6] Remember, it is the last image they will have of the dance. Take a moment to consider the important distinction between stopping and ending: stopping is arbitrary, whereas ending is conclusive, decisive. A well-considered ending can resolve a dance, sum it all up, tie it together, or even make a commentary on it. Whatever its function, a dance shouldn't suddenly just stop, unless of course that is part of your intention. Of course there are as many ways of ending as there are dances. Some of them are: reaching a high energy tour de force; creating a sense of cyclical closure (e.g., returning to opening material as in ABA); resolving the story line; or winding down to a quieting stillness.

Choreographic Study: Two Alternative Ends
Choreograph a study with two distinctly different endings. Show both studies. Perform each in its entirety.
   Discussion. It is interesting to note the point the choreographer identifies as "the beginning of the ending." Do the viewers agree with her? How did the different endings affect the impact and import of the dance itself?

When a dance is created for public performance, a bow needs to be considered. Although it is not an integral part of the dance, it warrants attention since it is an acknowledgment of the applause for that piece. The different possibilities range from a simple, formal bow to ones done in character with the piece itself, and from staged encores to no bow at all. Each of these may be as simple or elaborate as the choreographer chooses. Keep in mind that several may be called for, so set successive ones as well, possibly becoming shorter and simpler.

The finished, formed dance is an integrated statement. It functions as one complete whole. It is all about one thing, has a beginning, middle, end. No matter how complex, there is a simplicity in the overall statement. The overall form will be determined by the needs of the dance, whether it takes on a form that has been used many times before (a compositional structure) or derives its own unique one.

As a dance grows toward form, any of a number of things

may bring pressure to bear and help shape the overall structure. These can range from its dramatic inevitability to precomposed music. Yet the choreographer's intent remains the most intrinsic and therefore influential determinant of the final form. It is the integrating and focusing factor of the piece. As the needs of the dance are being met, the form unfolds. How does it need to begin? Where does it want to go? Where is the climax? What is the next most important part of the piece? How does it complete itself?

Improv: Overall Form

Improvise a longish rendering to one graph at a time, as though it is your score.

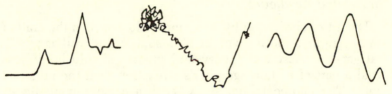

Choreographic Study: Graph-a-Dance

This requires you to attend to a piece in its larger context, paying less attention to the individual movements that you've been so intimately involved with during the creating and preliminary building stages. Create a solo study and draw a pictorial graph of its form which indicates: overall shape, number of sections, climax(es). Show the solos in small groups of four or five dancers. After each dance is finished the watchers draw a graph of it (do not try to capture each nuance; the graph is a big overview). Then the graphs are compared with the choreographer's. Discuss. Rework your dance based on feedback, striving for clarity of overall form. Show it again. This can also be done for some dances in repertory.

The usefulness of such graphs, whether visual or mental, is that they provide an overall perspective of the inception, growth, and resolution of the piece, and of the relationship between the parts. It makes the reminder about not leaving the end till the end even more significant and valid.

9 /
Abstraction

In Art and Aesthetics

The art of choreography is far more elusive than the craft of choreography, and it involves philosophical as well as practical aspects. Aesthetic theory and process should be no less vital a part of a choreographer's education than the nuts and bolts. The choreographer works with a heavily symbolic art form. Since all symbols are abstractions, creating dances implicitly involves the process of abstracting. (Actually you have been abstracting in all the choreographic work you have done thus far.)

In art, each perceiver imaginatively grasps the symbolic abstraction that the artist puts forth. The specific meaning of the art work (symbol) is not set or consensually agreed upon. It is expected that each viewer will interpret it from his own frame of reference. In everyday speech, the word *chair* (an abstract word-symbol) identifies a class of objects that share common properties; in art, we are concerned with one specific chair, its color, shape, how it may be sat upon, moved.

Art comes from the breaks, rifts, euphoria, and gouges that perforate all experience. According to the temperament of the particular artist, varying degrees of cognitive craft and technique are employed in giving these aesthetic form. The process—the rumblings becoming poetic, soft temporal transitions evolving to create a continuous whole—is a process of abstraction.

To abstract is to remove, separate from, condense, distill the essence of. Art isolates and refines such essences from life. There is no intention to copy external reality. From a morass, from a comprehensive macrocosmic world, the artist singles out a specific facet and works with it, exploring its subtleties and shadings, organically forms it, and presents it to the viewer.

The artist's task is to pull some essential aspect out of life and isolate it, thus forcing attention on it. This process involves a certain trade-off, in that some of the surrounding (and connotative) information is lost, but the focal point is perceived with greater clarity than previously possible. It is analogous to seeing an entire landscape and a distant tree within it—and then looking only at that same tree through a close-up lens. Another trade-off is that while abstraction in some ways loses information, in others it bridges the chasms left by real experience and provides new workable connections for the viewer.

Abstraction is not a device such as those we were working with in the last chapter. It is a philosophical construct of a process. However, in order to be realized, it needs such devices. Each artist has his own filtering system in which these tools get used. How he uses them to create, combine, exchange, mold, and produce images and image systems is determined by style preferences, visions, and intentions.

Any abstraction contains the essence of an image, feeling, or idea, and conveys the artist's intent at some level of perception—sometimes obviously, sometimes subtly. Representational or not, obtuse or mimetic, a successful dance reaches some connection, touches some sentience within, such that you can see the dance and *know* in your gut what it is about even though you may not be able to *say* what it is that you know so clearly.

Such an identifiable essence is the aspect that imprints most clearly on the brain. It relates to experience and thus is easily registered in the tacit knowledge storehouse. By speaking directly to your experience, an essence is intuitively felt, understood. This is precisely the type of communication that art seeks to achieve. This mode of knowing—holistic-sensory-immediate—is a natural place for synesthesia to occur, allowing us to feel muscular tension when viewing certain arrangements of paint on canvas, to have a sensory recall when watching a modern dance work or ballet, to see motion or colors when listening to music.

Particularly in the art of dance, we are inundated with all kinds of kinesthetic responses. This is due in part to the strong identification we have with the medium of dance, the human body. Because of this, it is one of the least abstract of the arts, as is drama. Music is usually considered to be the most abstract, yet within its repertory there is a wide range, from absolute music which has no narrative or literal reference, to program music, which is usually directly linked to a specific event or story line. But even the most emotive dance abstracts to some degree, because it *is* dance, an art form, and thus different from life. Modern dance has made use of a wide range of abstraction, from highly emotional message dances to the fantastic images created by Nikolais. When the emphasis is on pure movement or design as opposed to dramatic content, dance thus becomes capable of a fairly high degree of abstraction. The more a dance is abstracted, the more it is characterized by pure movement, by qualities, timing, line, and shape—at the expense of plot, emotional overtones, or representational images. Balanchine's *Agon* is one of the finest examples of such abstract dance. When props or costumes are added that extend or camouflage the natural body shape, more abstraction is obtained. But even in the most abstract dance, there is no getting away from the humanness of the dancer.

Dance abstracts from behavior, tangible things, gestures, other works of art, images, emotions, symbols, stories, pedestrian movement et al. Regardless of which of these is being abstracted, the process remains the same—the choreographer singles out specific aspects that she wishes to focus on and attends to those in terms of movement, while not attending to its other real (but to her, less important) denotations and connotations. That which the choreographer defines as the essence is made intense, vivid, larger than life, so much so that an entire dance can be built around it.

Imagery

An image may be private or universal, charged with emotional, visual, metaphorical, or ideational overtones or not. While being quite specific, it often has broad implications and calls forth a whole family of related images. Usually the image itself is not in movement terms but may be translated into movement terms.

> *Improv: Mother and Child*
> ◊ You are a mother with a child. Find ways to hold, rock, feed, play with, support, love your child. Involve the images in movement. Explore different ways of opening up the image (rock the child on the back of your leg). Use fantasy or surreal "child" surrogates and situations (the child as a floating balloon, or twice the size of the mother, or shapes giving birth to other shapes). . . . Now you are the child being played with, supported, rocked, fed, snuggled. . . .

> *Choreographic Study: Mother and Child*
> Create two studies using the mother and child image: one that is quite representational, wherein the images are easily recognizable, and one in which the movement (or design) takes over and becomes predominant (a solo of being rocked, variations on holding and feeding). In the second study, the image is used without direct reference to the literal; it is used abstractly as pure movement, pure design.

The above makes use of a relationship as its image. Another type of image that could serve as motivation would be a tangible object. Even a timeworn and badly used image like "be a tree" can be successful if dealt with in movement terms. The next improv and follow-up discussion shows how this is achieved using a candle as the image to be worked with.

Improv: Candle

♀ A candle, a flame . . . flickering. The candle has many wicks. Some of the flames may be sparking or sputtering. (Remember to use all parts of your body for the various movement qualities.) The wax is melting, heavily, sluggishly. The shape changes, softens; there's a loss of definition. Work with the flickering in one part of your body and the melting in another. As the candle melts it takes on many different shapes—long and elegant, gnarled and scary. A drop of wax starts to roll down the candle, spills, picks up speed, then rolls onto the floor and hardens. Clusters of drippings form surrealistic shapes. Mix the images. Play with them any way they work for you.

There are many aspects of an image, too many to use successfully at one time. Some are impossible or impractical for movement; others are not relevant. Using the image of the burning candle, let's analyze it to see how we arrived at the above improv. We chose to concentrate on two opposing movement qualities—flickering (quick, light) and melting (slow, heavy). Melting emphasizes gravity while flickering yields levity. The loss of definition and change of shape in the wax motivates changes in the use of space. The drop of wax image allowed for a contrasting use of speed. We disregarded those things that cannot easily be directly translated into movement: size, color, heat. Similar analysis could be done for any image to help formulate an improv or find a starting place for a dance.

Exploratory Work: Image Gathering

Make a list of illusions, things, relationships, or ideas that could work as movement images. Choose two and analyze them into those aspects you would use as the main focus, the contrasting material, and those you would discard.

Selection is the key. As you select and discard different aspects of the image, you are abstracting. In real life you would probably never analyze in such detail, or would you? or do you? intuitively? automatically?

Choreographic Study: Abstracting an Image
Create a study based on one of the images you analyzed.

Animate images are often used for abstraction. Because of their inherent movement characteristics they are somewhat easier to analyze than inanimate objects. The danger is that translation into dance can be overly literal. In order to provide a richer bed of movement stimuli, it pays to go into detail with the image.

Exploratory Work
Look at nature movies, copies of *National Geographic*, and Disney cartoons of animals. Pick an animal to work with—an alligator, spider, monkey, kangaroo, rattlesnake, tarantula. What movement qualities make him distinct? How does he eat, run, fight, play, clean himself? Does he have a tail? How does he use it? Is he nervous or calm, a hunter or the hunted, a pack animal or loner, a runner or freezer, climber or crawler? What is the texture of his skin? How many legs? What are his archetypal personality traits?

Improv: Wild Kingdom
Work with the various aspects of your animal. ⟡ Begin . . .

Thus far we have been focusing on the use of abstraction with images of relationships, objects, and animals; but much choreographic work abstracts from human movement itself.

Gestures

The purpose of choreographic movement is to produce dynamic images, to create impressions—impressions of line or form, of meaning or beauty or pain. That type of movement is quite different from daily practical movements which accomplish tasks, indicate needs, or communicate information. None of us intends to produce artistic movements when mixing concrete, or saluting, or sticking out our tongues; such behaviors are goal-oriented and have purposes unto themselves. But in any such movements there are wonderful visual "goings on" if one seeks and notices them.

This the choreographer must do like a detective, seeing and discovering things that otherwise go assumed, unnoticed, or ignored. He zeroes in on all the basic and complex, ordinary and spectacular movement that operates the ongoing train of life—actions, gestures, behaviors. These human movements are among the basic sources the choreographer uses in the process of abstraction. It is imperative that he cultivate his visual acuity and see things which other people do not notice.

Gestures are a major part of such daily movement. As physical movement symbols that express or emphasize ideas and emotions, they are the most overt and commonly shared language of the body. Although they accompany speech as a way of emphasizing what is being said, they function independently as well. Indeed, people often resort to the use of gesture when they do not speak the same language, and in so doing, can communicate a tremendous wealth of information.

Although gestures have specific meanings of their own, their real power and meaning comes from the bodily and facial expressions that accompany them. Birdwhistell warns that no body position or movement in and of itself has a precise meaning.[1] Interestingly enough, gestures seem to retain their commonly understood meaning only in conjunction with appropriate facial and other body clues and may be colored, altered, or contradicted by subtle shadings and differences. For instance, an open palm may mean: (1) "I have no weapons, I come in peace," (2) begging for alms, (3) a polite "after you" when going through a door or getting in line.

The hands ("V for Victory," thumbing a ride) and face (wink

or nod) are the main, but certainly not the only, parts of the body used in gesturing (a nudge with an elbow, a bow). Kissing or hugging would be classed as movement, rather than as gesture, whereas pursing one's lips may expressively run the gestural gamut and indicate anything from a tender endearment to a lewd invitation, depending on the slightest variation of how it is done and what other behavior accompanies it. The more we try to focus on gesture, the more we must realize that expression, as a sister behavior, is inexorably tied up with it; and that they mutually coexist and drastically affect one another.

Short & to the Point
Pick a gesture. Perform it with the following attitudes in the body and face: (1) with the usual intent of the gesture, (2) contrary to the usual intent of the gesture, (3) with a neutral attitude.

Other daily movements, less clearly defined but intuitively understood, fall into the category of mannerisms: twitches, playing with hair or beard, readjusting clothes, smoking, fussing with worry beads. Often these are outlets for nervous energy.

Exploratory Work: Gestures
Make a list of gestures. Take a few and describe the different meanings that they could yield depending on changes in context, facial or postural expression, etc.

Improv: Gestural Trigger and Response
Make up an original gesture for each of the following four meanings: greeting, curse, blessing, self-protection. ∮ A group of six or more begin milling around, passing by but not touching one another. Every so often you may use one of your gestures toward someone else. They in turn respond with appropriate movement. Allow the interaction to complete itself as it needs to. You may repeat or alter the intitiating gesture to

evoke a slightly different response or you may use any of your other pre-set, self-created gestures that seem appropriate. Your encounter may be short or may take time to develop. When it is complete, continue milling and pursue another encounter. Use different gestures as they seem fitting.

Discussion. Were your gestures easily understood? If not, why? Were they misinterpreted or unintelligible? Was one gesture particularly unsuccessful in being understood? How would you change it? How were you at reading other people's gestures? Did you find yourself restating the initial gesture in the movement interaction that followed? Developing or abstracting it? Why do you think that happened?

When gestures are used as a movement motif and developed, (see pp. 101–07), they become abstractions and a rich resource for the choreographer. As such they lie somewhere outside or in between the realms of drama, mime, and dance.

Choreographic Study: Gesture Development
Choose a standard gesture. Experiment with manipulating it as a motif. Create a study, using that material as the primary resource.

The choreographer can work with gesture in two ways: (1) she may incorporate/or abstract *established* gestures, or (2) she may *create* gestures that become meaningful within the context of a given work. The aim of such created gesture symbols is that they be perceived and understood on an intuitive level (and perhaps on a cognitive level as well).

Sign language, in attempting to communicate directly, uses abstraction. Many of the gestures are as beautiful as they are expressive and succinct. The National Theater of the Deaf uses both the type of abstraction inherent in signing and the tools of expressive dramatic abstraction basic to acting. Mime, as another art form, also has made use of abstraction to develop instantly recognizable re-creations of reality (the wall, walking up stairs). Sign and mime both provide a wealth of material that would be excellent as additional resources for the choreographer.

Degrees of Abstraction

Art creates illusions and presents perceptions that relate to sentience. The images created by the process of abstraction may be fairly concrete (in that their referents are easily identifiable) or not. When they are not, the result is labeled *abstract* (abstruse or nonrepresentational). So you can have an abstract abstraction or, for that matter, a literal abstraction.

> *Choreographic Study: Five Degrees of Abstraction*
> Take any image and manipulate it so that you have five very short movement versions, each more abstract, each further away from the conventional, but all keeping the essence of the image. You will have five degrees of abstraction. The first will be very representational. The last is highly abstract and removed from the original and may not be easily recognizable; but the spirit is there, and at some level of perception (no matter how subliminal) a connection can be make to the original image. Make a phrase using all five degrees, starting with the fifth degree and progressing back through the fourth, third, second, first, to the original.

Different degrees of abstraction are often used within a single dance. In *Swan Lake* both extremes are used: pantomime emphasizes the dramatic line while abstract or pure dance is used in solo, pas de deux, and some of the corps work with little or no relation to the story. In *Moor's Pavanne*, *Frontier*, and *Rodeo*, pure movement, gesture, and images interplay, each being abstracted to varying degrees. Other dances have characters but lack a plot, narrative, or sense of causality; in these, the choreographer can be poet and not storyteller.

Pure Dance

Often a dance is devoid of an outside identifiable reference. It is simply a dance, pure dance, consisting of abstract movement. This is dance for its own sake, its own intrinsic flow, excitement, satisfaction ... the celebration of moving in form ... the classic opening numbers ... the numerous Vivaldi pieces. People just love to just dance, and other people just love to just watch people just dancing! So the message is often ... *Dance.*

Sometimes when people refer to "abstract dance" they are talking about pure dance, dance that is characterized by design that is geometric. In such a piece the interest is in the lines, designs, shapes, and movement of the bodies and not in their emotional content or dramatic intention.

Choreographic Study: Pure Dance
Create a pure dance.

As we have seen, *abstract* as differentiated from *abstraction* refers to movement that is mainly characterized by design or form and can help define or characterize a style, approach, or preference in art, for example, the style of Nikolais and Balanchine as distinct from Sokolow, Limón, or Helen Tamiris.

Romanticism / Classicism

The great periods in art tend to come under the rubric of one of two major approaches, the two extremes of romanticism and classicism. (Classical with a small *c* describes *an approach to art* that embodies objectivity, formality, balance, simplicity, and dignity. This approach reflects the Greek and Roman ideals. Artists have used a classical approach to their specific media over the centuries. When a whole group of artists in one culture approach a specific media classically it may be called Classical with a capital *C*, e.g., the Classical Period of music is from 1750 to 1820.) Classicism shares many characteristics with abstract art, while romanticism is identified by its more concrete and representational approach. Romanticism "is spontaneous and demands participation of its audience, where classicism is reflective and invites observation. It is in effect emotional where classicism is mental; it induces excitement instead of balanced admiration; it is energetic and exuberant where classicism is poised and orderly; it seeks to awaken sympathetic experience instead of the combination of aesthetic responses that is generally described as beauty."[2]

> *Discussion.* Looking at the works of past and present choreographers, identify each as having a romantic or classic approach.

Abstraction vs. Stylization

There is one final point that needs to be made concerning abstraction: it is often confused with stylization. To clear this up, let us return for a moment to the introductory remarks on the discussion of gesture in which we said that the most obvious thing of all to abstract would be movement itself. Even when an ordinary movement is not the image chosen for abstraction, it nevertheless gets abstracted in the process. Walking, a pedestrian and mundance movement, is probably the richest single source of locomotor movement used by dancers. One could emphasize the height, speed, or size of a walk; one could deal with its physical components (the heels, bent or straight knees, the arm swing); one could focus on the placement, movement, or design of the rest of the body. Each of these would result in a different abstraction of a walk. But—and this is an important distinction—they would *not* each result in a different stylization of a walk. You could do three abstractions of a walk: (1) a knee walk, (2) a walk with chest thrust forward, and (3) a very fast followed by a very slow walk. Yet all three could be in the style of a marching soldier or of a Victorian lady with a bustle, or of any other character you choose. Abstraction and style are not the same thing; they operate independently of one another.

10 /
Style

Style is the signature of an individual, group, or entire culture at a specific period in time. A movement style is a recurrent or qualitatively patterned way of moving, an identifiable manner or mode of physical expression. Movement styles are determined by many factors: historical time frames, personality, body type, cultural values. Primitive people, for example, often emphasize rhythm and time, while Wigman and Nikolais are fascinated with space, each in quite different ways and with different results.

To help develop a knowledge and awareness of style useful for the choreographer we will consider the following six categories: (1) personal movement style—an individual's movement personality, his movement signature; (2) choreographic style—the composite of personal and artistic preferences that characterizes the mode, manner, and content of one's choreography; (3) codified technique—a personal style that becomes refined and classified to the point where a movement vocabulary builds up around it (as Graham, Humphrey-Weidman, or Hawkins technique), sometimes the result of coupling personal movement style with a theory of movement; (4) theories of movement—an identified theory or model that uses one basic phenomenon as the source and propelling force for movement; (5) cultural style—movement patterns that embody the attitudes and values of a given age or culture; (6) great periods in art—stylistic approaches epitomized by certain historical periods in the evolution of the fine arts.

Study of each category should be part of the choreographer's education. They provide insight into self and into the heritage of dance; they focus attention on the recognizable stylizations of some of the great choreographers as well as on diverse cultural and artistic trends; they look at how, and to what extent, the cultural values of a given period direct the course of art over the span of many years; finally, they provide an excellent source of experiences to seed and broaden the emerging choreographer's own development of style.

Although there are a number of ways to facilitate this development, it must start from and be based on a healthy respect for the different ways individuals move, respond, and feel about movement. This is, after all, one of the cornerstones upon which the modern dance movement was founded and built, and which has enabled its contemporary evolution. So we encourage natural individual differences rather than thwarting them. We suggest applications and uses of these differences and ways for you to capitalize on your individuality, reminding you to use your distinctive qualities as a primary and very special resource.

We'll try to open an awareness to your own and others' styles by calling for specific observations. This can help bring your inherent (though perhaps latent) perceptiveness to a conscious level. Once aware of your individual style, you can develop it to a fuller realization. This can be done via feedback on your choreographic studies, or in individually tailored projects that will help you probe more deeply into a particular aspect. Such probing may help you identify and shape your trademark, your own element of movement distinction.

Example: Since you move so easily in an electric, liquid way, why don't you find out how you can move that way through space with quite a fast traveling pace; use that quality in a stationary position; on the floor; play with it in different parts of your body; find three contrasting qualities that make it stand out. Using what you found, make a dance study.

The work in this chapter will add breadth as well as depth by getting you to observe and move in other styles. At the same time you're discovering your own uniqueness, you'll need to watch others discovering theirs and become more aware of the similarities and differences. You'll see other styles, discuss, and learn to articulate verbally what you see, and you'll become capable of recognizing your teacher's style for what it is, her style, and that it is not the only way to move. Experiences, improvs, and choreographic studies will let you experiment in the different stylistic categories reinforcing the idea that this increased breadth can be utilized for your own solo choreography, for performing someone else's works, or for choreographing on someone with a different style than your own.

Personal Movement Style

In modern dance, personal movement style was the starting point for producing the codified techniques that exist today; as such it has been more important than historical style. The insistence on personal approach is undeniably the single factor most responsible for the very existence of modern dance itself, thanks to Isadora Duncan. So, helping develop a strong but flexible personal movement style is essential if we are to foster the emergence of the individually creative artist.

A person's style includes, but is more than, his typical movements. It is a badge of distinction when it becomes an artist's hallmark; a movement rut when the movements are overused and stand in the way of finding new material.

A person's movement style is always uniquely expressive of the whole person. It is the way you move—a result of how you feel, perceive, and respond to your world, to others, and to yourself—and therefore it determines the way you will create in movement. Your personal movement style as a dancer is influenced by, and is as basic as, body structure (shape, size), type of dance training, personality, and individual space/time/ energy preferences. A person's style is delimiting, but need not be restrictive (although it can be, as in the well-known rut). It is, according to Valerie Hunt, a "central tendency from which you deviate in both directions."

A realistic self-image is essential to the developing choreographer's artistic as well as psychological health. You need to be able to see yourself as you really are; this facilitates personal objectivity, identification, and growth. A self-image includes mental, social, emotional, and physical aspects. In relation to the education of the choreographer, we're dealing with a rather complex body image. It includes the visual physical attributes (tall, skinny, long-limbed), natural abilities (easy stretch, poor elevation, good sense of timing), and space/time/ energy affinities (big mover, slow, gentle). These must be identified, accepted, acknowledged.

The fact that function and form intermesh and are cross-influential is particularly evident in natural states—scale affects movement. A swan, one of the largest flying birds, needs a long runway, and its takeoff is lumbering; the small hummingbird can rise vertically and hover in one place. There are flying fish, squirrels, insects—each with a form uniquely suited and adapted to achieving aerodynamic principles in different ways. Similarly, people's size and shape are an important determinant in how they move. It is all wrong for a short, dynamic mover to try and take for his own the style of his softly flowing, long-limbed teacher, although it is useful for him to explore that way of moving to help widen his own range.

Each of us is more compatible with some kinds of movement than with others. Identifying your affinities doesn't limit you to those, but lets you consciously make the best use of them. It lets you understand that the difficulty in performing some things is not a singular result of ineptitude, but rather that, perhaps, it is just not your natural way of moving—and therefore requires more work to achieve the desired results. Finding out what you need work on (and what you already have that is waiting to be released) seems to be a realistic and intelligent, as well as efficient, way to go about becoming versatile.

The following exercise provides a fine initial foray into observation and identification of personal movement style, and serves as an introduction to this area.

Exploratory Work

Each person thinks up some physical activity to teach the group or have them do (anything from jumping rope to juggling). Bring any necessary equipment. It doesn't matter if it's a skill, a sport, or some form of physical labor. Divide the group in half, and while one person explains or teaches the activity to one half, the rest will observe. Observers should watch for differences in how the participating movers use space, time, or force. All the participants will be receiving the same instructions, watching the same person demonstrate. Rotate leaders, so the observers will see the movers in a variety of situations. Within a very brief time, it will become evident that some of the movers consistently use larger (or smaller) amounts of space, are more relaxed, expend less energy, move faster, etc., regardless of whether they're involved in an activity they're familiar with, skilled at, or not. These consistencies constitute the gross and most easily identifiable movement characteristics that form part of their personal movement style and have a keen effect on it. Stay at an objective level as though collecting data, for this is what it is. The emphasis is on what is happening, not whether it is clumsy/pretty, right/wrong, sucessful/unsuccessful. Be sure that this is clear before beginning. Switch roles: movers observe and visa versa.

A check list is another useful tool in helping dancers identify personal affinities in movement. Which movements feel most comfortable? What things do you do easily or first when solving a movement problem? What are your particular movement affinities and tendencies? Take time with this list.

Personal Movement Style Check List

1. What are your movement idiosyncracies? (Lovely Lady, Puck's Surprise, Angel of Doom, Flying Machine, etc.)
2. What are your favorite ways of using space, time, energy? (See relevent chapters for specifics.)
3. Do you prefer to travel or stay in place?
4. Are you impulsive or sure and steady?
5. Would you characterize your movements as more gestural (existing in the limbs or periphery) or postural (involving a lot of use of the torso)?

If you are familiar with the movement classifications of a particular system, such as Effort/Shape, it would be helpful and wise to evaluate yourself according to that terminology as well.

Improv: Student-Set Improv in Personal Movement Style
After answering the above check list, structure an improv that would epitomize your movement style and preferences (e.g., lyric and loose, using a lot of space, very gestural in the arms). Improvise on your own self-set structure.

Choreographic Study: Self-Style
Either using your own improv as source and point of departure or beginning anew, create a short study in personal movement style—a typical "you" dance. Working in partners, teach your study to another. All studies are then shown individually by the dance learner—the creator sitting out. Everyone tries to guess whose it is. Then it is repeated with the creator-choreographer dancing it right along with his partner. The goal is two-fold: (1) forcing the choreographer to hone in on the quintessence, the absolute core of his style, and (2) demanding that the observer keenly distinguish between the person doing the movement and the movement style itself.

At some point, discuss each individual's style. This discussion can come before or after the Self-Style choreographic study. At first, some dancers think they do not have a style, but they're usually delighted when the rest of the group actually does indentify and define one. Having to choreograph in your style after the class discusses this can be frustrating because of the limits seemingly imposed by the labels others have tagged you with. This frustration is good; it pays to discuss it. These labels are descriptions of how others see you— so maybe it's time to enlarge your range, develop your style, fulfill your potential and not live in restrictive labels or get caught by the typecasting. Some people are surprised by how they're perceived. Use your own and others' analysis as a place to go and grow from. From the insight gained in the discussions, consider how to make the most of your strong points and avoid your movement clichés. Become acquainted with and deal with your weaknesses. (This is, of course, an ever-ongoing responsibility shared by self and teacher.)

Choreographic Study: Atypical Style
Design and set an improv for yourself that's the opposite of, and in contrast to, your preferred movement style. Improvise on this, as before. From this, create a study in Atypical Style—a "that's not me!" dance. (The level of success in this study is commensurate with the amount of frustration produced in creating and performing it.)

A distinctive personal movement style can either be helpful or harmful. It's an impairment when it becomes limiting, a dead end, a closed box. Yet this selfsame style, when used as a starting place, can give a sense of identity, of home base from which to explore. The resulting surety of self frees one to wander far and wide. Think of it as an access, a key to many doors, an I ("eye") that can visualize a grand multiplicity of images; then it is vital and helpful. It is perhaps a truism that every artist has a unique and identifiable personal style—but it is the great artist who is able to apply that style to a broad range of modes, themes, periods (as Picasso's Representational, Blue, Primitive, Cubist periods).

If you want to choreograph for someone else in their style you can (1) set it straight out from what you know and have seen of her style; (2) identify her movement characteristics and improvise by yourself on those, drawing on material from your improvisational interpretation of them; or (3) structure an improv and have her do it, then decide what material you want to keep and develop for her. When a choreographer has a dancer improvise and sets it from that, less of the choreographer's style and more of the dancer's style comes through. Choreographing from her improvisational movements demands that you keep carefully clear of her favorite movements, her ruts. She's already done that dance; that's hers, not yours. Try to see a potential in her that she has not fully explored, and help her widen her range.

Choreographic Study: For Someone Else
Choreograph for someone, making new use of her personal style.

In watching Susan doing the "essence of Susan" dance as choreographed by Dave, one sees Susan as intended but also Dave's choreographic style. Have the class guess who choreographed it. Also ask the performer how it felt; was it "her"?

Choreographic Style

As you choreograph many dances you develop a choreographic style. You begin to find yourself and the mode and manner best suited to your creative expression. Over time, that style becomes richer and more subtle. It incorporates your personal movement style plus many other factors that influence the dancer-choreographer. These factors include: feelings; attitudes; modes of creating (intellectual vs. intuitive, the mind vs. the muscle); preferred working relationships (solos, small or large groups); values of art and aesthetic judgments; preferences for inner or outer stimuli; degree of abstraction;

approaches that are conservative or avant garde, dramatic or abstract, motional or emotional, literal or symbolic; preference for working improvisationally or with set choreography. All of these and more constitute your choreographic style from which you will make dances. It is "that peculiar personal rapport which has developed between an artist and his medium."[1]

Often, one can look at a dance and know who the choreographer is. The movement signature is unmistakeable. After just a little bit of exposure, hardly anyone would confuse a work by Limón for one by Twyla Tharp or Nikolais. What distinguishes a great artist is that no matter how distinctive his style is, he keeps developing and expanding it. Anna Sokolow says, "I see no reason to fight a personal language; it's an organic statement of the person. But one must not rest on it. The important thing is to stretch the personal vocabulary so that it does not remain static. This does not mean changing its essential nature. One can remain one's self without repeating a statement."[2] Martha Graham is a prime example. Over the years her choreography evolved through many varied periods (Americana, Greek tragedy) while her individual style has remained constant. Doris Humphrey's choreographic style confirmed a resolutely optimistic viewpoint. Pauline Koner, in speaking of Humphrey, says, "She never resolved her pieces on a negative note. No matter how desperate the material was, the resolution was positive. She always said she believed in the wonder of the human spirit.[3]

The education of a painter traditionally includes learning the techniques of the masters—Rembrandt, Monet, Van Gogh—not of one, but of several. This training encourages historical perspective; it provides exposure to, and actual experience in, widely differentiated yet highly formed styles, ones that have influenced the state of the art in its development to the present day; it allows the student to begin to realize points of personal identification and points of departure. These same advantages are waiting for the dancer, and that is why we suggest that choreographic training include the opportunity to get to know and dabble in the styles of some of the great artists in the dance world.

Exploratory Work: Major Choreographers

Look at pictures and movies of some of the major choreographers (ideally, several of their works) and discuss their respective styles. Try to identify the significant elements, the choreographer's distinguishing features. Try it with stills (photographs, slides, or drawings, as of Duncan) as well as with films. See several films and live performances. Find and identify the threads, the identifiable earmarks of a given choreographer's work.

Improv: Imitation

Note: This will work only if you have had some exposure to choreographers' works via live performance or film.

Now that you have identified some choreographic styles, improvise in the style of several major choreographers. If applicable, use contributory effects (Cage's music, when working on Cunningham, or fabric stretch bags when focusing on Nikolais). Try to include the works of people who are substantially different from one another (Duncan, Graham, Limón, Tharp, Halprin).

Choreographic Study: In Imitation of a Great Choreographer

Compose a short dance based on any famous choreographer's style. Decide on a theme that would be most typical, or that would exemplify the style most easily. [This usually turns out to be a stereotyping or a satire—that's fine.] Keep it short to make the point and have an impact.

Repeat this exercise using the work of several different choreographers. If time is limited (as it always seems to be), do it in abbreviated fashion, so the choreographic study is quite short, perhaps no more than fifteen or twenty seconds. The important thing is exposure and experimentation in an alternate mode, giving you a chance to "get a feel for it." Vary the repeats of the assignment by doing it sometimes independently, sometimes in groups or pairs.

Imitation is not, of course, the end goal. What we are aiming to do is build you into a choreographer who is better versed in the aesthetic roots of your art and get you to experiment with movement and choreographic approaches that are alien to anything you'd ordinarily produce yourself.

Codified Technique

When there is enough excitement, vitality, and creativity in an artist to engender an enthusiastic following, and when the technical aspects of the movement style are developed, classified, and refined, a personal movement style may become a codified technique. Such a technique makes it possible for others to adopt the style and take on the nuances that make it unique. It provides a way for dancers to become articulate in that movement idiom. The technique embodies the theories in identifiable movements and ways of moving and ideally combines them with intelligent principles of anatomy and kinesiology. The technique is composed of short, easily learned patterns that can be assimilated and built on. It allows dancers to speak with clarity through a movement style that is not their own and lets them work in harmony within a group.

Modern dance today is often taught through a technique that has evolved from one particular person's style, that is, a codified technique. This is efficient because it trains people to perform that particular dancer's choreography with clarity and skill and gives experience in a viable theory of movement. However, when used exclusively, it is not the ideal method for developing individual artists or providing a creatively rich dance education. Students can get stuck in it to the point where it becomes their way of responding. For example, if we described Graham's style as predominantly strong, grounded, sharp (angular or percussive), bold—and a student had been schooled strictly in this technique, that would form her major reservoir of kinesthetic and choreographic movement. She'd tend to speak with her body in only that language, with that dialect or inflection. Yet it would be a superimposed rather than an internal style—more "hairdo" than "blood type."

It is one thing for the dancer who is solely performance-oriented, whose single goal is to join a specific company and concentrate on performing the works of a particular choreographer, to focus on and train his body in one technique only. But for most modern dance students, and certainly for the serious choreographer, this is not the case. Dancers go from company to company. Companies draw their repertory from a wide variety of new and well-established choreographers. No, there's nothing wrong with learning a technique—as long as it's not the only one, and it is learned in conjunction with an approach that helps you get to know your own "blood type." As a choreographer, don't restrict yourself in any dance experience: explore; learn what you can from different teachers; then go on to find the essence of your own movement and choreographic style.

Theories of Movement

Often a codified technique is based on some theory that singles out and uses a particular phenomenon as the motivating source for movement. We'll explore through improvisation the theories of movement on which two of the predominant styles in modern dance are based. The idea is to explore your movement response to the theory, not to try and imitate how another has realized that theory on his body. These improvs should not reproduce the style of the choreographer who initially developed them, but should demonstrate the process of developing a style from a central theory, the theory having been found or identified through improvisation and experimentation.

These theories of movement can be seen as fundamentals or core motivators. Contraction and release, for example, is the central movement idea of Graham's technique. It is also the basis of many primitive movement styles and the resulting evolution to jazz. This shows how different styles can come out of the same basic movement theory.

Work experimentally with each theory as would a novice, as though you had never heard of it or its creator before. The Graham contraction, highly refined and stylized, is just one of many that contraction and release, as a theory of movement, could lead to.

Improv: Contraction and Release
◊ Make your body as condensed, tight, as possible. Slowly release the tension and then expand even further, getting air between all the fibers in your body. Try it again a different way . . . again in a twisted fashion. Pick one part of your body and find different ways of contracting and expanding it. Try it in various parts of your body. Vary the speed, sometimes contract fully, sometimes partially. Try sole of the foot, side of the ribs, back of neck, palm of the hand, abdomen. Try having it start at the neck and proceed down to the tail and vice versa. The center of the contraction and release can be in two places simultaneously. Find a way to let a condensing and expanding take you to the floor, to standing, through space on various levels. Play with contractions and releases—rhythmically, lyrically, and dramatically (being burned, contracting shyly away from a caress, expanding in a laugh). Remember it can be a partial contraction or release. How can it make you turn, fall and recover, propel you through space, go into the air (leap, skip, jump)?

Choreographic study: Contraction and Release
Create a study based on contraction and release gleaned from the above improv.

The motivating theory for Humphrey was termed the "Arc Between Two Deaths." The arc is analogous to life, with each end of the arc representing death. She viewed the equilibrium of standing still or lying down as deathlike, while the struggle against gravity (resulting in fall, recovery, and suspension) was seen as life, action, and the stuff of dance—the arc. This was paralleled by a second image—the one of Apollo (philosophical, calm, rational, balanced, serene) and Dionysus (adventurous, dangerous, drunk), and man's struggle between the two, between stability and progress.[4]

Improv: Fall and Recovery
(Here again, respond to the theory as creatively as possible, not trying to come up with Humphrey's movement style.) ⚥ Standing, centered, erect, serene, no movement—a death. Begin to feel the movement within standing still, the little corrections for balance. Let them grow into a fluid shifting, a flexible sway. Let the movements increase till you lose your balance and you need to move to recover it—movement, life. Play with moving in and out of the stasis or balance of standing still. Find that moment of hesitation when you are off balance but not yet falling, the suspension before the fall through space. Try the balance, suspension, fall and recovery with different parts of the body (head, arm, hips) as the main initiator of the fall. Use the energy/momentum of the fall to initiate more movement—a role, rebound, recovery. It keeps moving you through space, to the floor and up again (a roll-suspension-roll-suspension is a natural outcome). It takes you into a turn, into elevation. Be on a swing or a trampoline. Move like a bouncing ball, a pendulum. Let the falls become heavier; you are losing your fight against gravity; it drags you lower and lower, until you give in, becoming passive, still.

Choreographic Study: Suspension, Fall and Recovery
⚥ Compose a study in which suspension, fall, and recovery are the sources of movement.

Each of these modern dance greats created her own theory of movement: for Isadora, it was that inspiration and movement came from the solar plexus; for Graham, the contraction and release; for Humphrey, the arc between two deaths. The latter two resulted in a codified technique, whereas Isadora's (although she certainly had an avid following) did not. Her legacy was not technical because her drive and inspiration were not technically oriented. In contrast, we have someone like Cunningham, whose movement rests on no single movement theory or priority, and yet whose personal style did result in a well-known, respected, and identifiable codified technique. "I'm not concerned with a style of dancing. I'm concerned with training someone to move."[5] However, Cunningham does have a definite choreographic theory. One aspect of it, chance, is dealt with above (pp. 117–20).

> *Discussion.* Personal movement style, codified technique, and theories of movement . . . how are they related? Are some prerequisites for others? Are they naturally present in an individual or do they require development?

> *Exploratory Work and Improv: Theory of Movement*
> Invent a theory of movement. Put it in improv form and try it out with a group of dancers.

Cultural Style

Cultural style reflects the social customs, religious beliefs, and philosophical ideals of a specific group of people—their notions of beauty, good, desirability, power, truth, virtue. It is influenced by ethnic body type, by collective body image, and by environment. The national dances of a people are a refinement of their movement tendencies. It is seen in the streets and taverns (by the people), in the theaters (by the professionals), and in places of worship (by the shamans). Cultural style varies from the lyric dances of the Greek islands to the romping, fun-loving dances of Israel to the restrained dances of Bali. These dances evolved slowly over the centuries but in essence they continue to epitomize the cultural values of the people.

The dance of the United States has evolved at a fast pace in the twentieth century. Its dances range from square dancing and ballroom, which have somewhat held their own over the years, to such fad dances as the Charleston, jitterbug, and disco.

The choreographer can use any cultural style as raw material for choreography without trying to reproduce authentic ethnic movement. In making an artistic statement he is merely utilizing the flavor of a specific style (such as flamenco) within his own stylistic approach.

Exploratory Work
Pick a culture. Do a little background work on its history, cultural values, religion, and on its social, folk, classical, or ritual dances. Listen to the music or folk songs; read a myth or folktales.

Improv: Cultural Style
Work in movement with anything that intrigued you. Just dance to some of the music from that culture. Play with some of your ideas with the music as a background even if it is not the music you will eventually use.

Choreographic Study: Cultural Style
Develop your ideas into a study using music from that country.

Great Periods in Art

The history of art is characterized by different styles or periods. Western painting may be representational, Cubist, Impressionist (to mention just a few). Music may be Baroque or Romantic. These styles are determined by technique, approach, degree of abstraction. They are influenced by the value system operating in the society from which they emerge. But often it is the individual artist reacting to or against that society whose vision is the instigator of the style. That vision is occassionally ahead of its time but certainly born of it, for instance, Picasso's Cubism or Isadora's modern dance.

In the twentieth century, artists were making new beginnings. One way of doing this was to go back to primitive attitudes toward art (which are imbued with strength, intensity, and directness), and primitive attitudes toward life (magic, awe, an earthy and erotic realism). A dance in the primitive style would have movements that are sparse, direct, intense, awkward, unelaborated; they are lean, taut, animalistic, and full of wonder, naiveté, and mystery. We are not moving as primitive man did, for we really don't know how he moved. What we are doing is distilling the essence of primitiveness, working through our interpretation of "as if for the first time," and thus trying to achieve a primitive style and effect.

Exploratory Work: Primitive

Collect photographs of cave drawings, cliff dwellings, sketches of prehistoric animals, dinosaurs, drawings showing the evolution of man. Find drum and tribal music, primitive artifacts, omens, children's drawings. Look at some examples of primitive style in art: Klee (child primitive), Gauguin (romantic primitive), Picasso, Modigliani (classical primitive), the German Expressionists (emotional primitive).

Improv: Early Man

[These directions are expressed in a conventionalized, "primitive" speech to help in setting the overall tone.] ϕ Begin on belly: let go. Feel earth. Be part of earth, like plant. Grow roots or seep into ground, water. Try joints, all joints—first time. Move around, feel space. Lift head. See new things. Crawl. Travel. Up to standing for first time . . . careful . . . balance . . . hard! See world from new place. Awkward!! Feel . . . see . . . wonder. Go. Drunk with delight. Run, like child. Fall . . . run again. Speed . . . space . . . slow . . . balance . . . reach. See flying thing. What is it? You try; try to fly. Catch and take into self that which flies. It dies. First death . . . ritual burial . . . prayer to appease gods.

Choreographic Study: Primitivism

Using any primitive image, create a study in primitivism.

Supplementary Group Improv in Primitivism

Refer to the Rhythm Circle improv (p. 68). Start at the point when the dancers are in a circle; have a drum give the rhythm. Give particular stress to the magic in the center of the circle.

In dance, we glean from styles in other arts those things that pertain to movement; we then create a dance in a parallel style. When choreographic works partake of or are based on any of the historical periods in art, the choreographer should become well acquainted with the literature, music, art, and drama of that period so as to impart a unified flavor to the work. That kind of care and attention can help in producing works which are as complete in their various aspects as is *Parade*—in which Léonide Massine drew on his contemporaries Picasso, Erik Satie, and Jean Cocteau who, each within his own medium, shared elements of a single style.

To explore these stylistic possibilities in class, the characteristics of the period should not be simply alluded to secondhand. The knowledge of the period should be as concrete as possible. By having a picture, record, or poem right there to see, hear, and get to know, your understanding of the style will be formed through multiple sensory input. You need to set the scene, to create an environment conducive to producing creative responses in that particular style. These styles are seen as they exist in their different mediums and are then translated into movement and design.

> *Improv/Choreographic Study: Great Periods in Art*
> There are many other styles—archaic, surrealist, etc. Try your hand at translating them to dance. Using Horst's *Modern Dance Forms in Relation to the Other Modern Arts*[6] as reference (or use Dali's paintings, Debussy's music, Egyptian art, Greek architecture), pick a style. Design an improv to explore it. Create a study from the improvised material.

A Pertinent Tangent

The next improv is a style-stretcher. Get out of your own way of moving. Get out of your teacher's way of moving. Try something different. A movement experience in strangeness can lead in many directions—to the grotesque or the fantastic, to distortions for purposes of psychological shock value, or to comic effect.

Improv: Strangeness

φ Begin a twisting or wringing movement; stress the asymmetrical design. When you find a particularly strange position, hold it for a few seconds, then continue and move on. Allow some staccato dabs to break into the twisting and held positions; their rhythm (timing) should be irregular, unpredictable, random. Include a shake, a vibration. What images are coming to mind? Insane, absurd, grotesque, distorted, gnarled, alien, funny. Use your image and continue to improvise.

Strangeness is a direct attempt to use the unusual, unexpected, distorted. It can lead to surprises, the alien, and unfamiliar. It is unclassical, unconventional, and at times becomes bizarre. This way of moving is a deviation from the natural and the usual. It is a distortion in space and design, in timing, and in the juxtaposition of energies (and qualities).

The material gleaned from this improv can be used sparsely, as contrast (a hint or shadow of other dimensions), or it can be the predominant factor for an entire piece.

Choreographic Study: Strangeness

Using an image from the improv and the movement elements of strangeness that support it, choreograph a study.

Discuss how the improv opened possibilities for the image. To what extent did it help you venture in new directions? What kinds of strangenesses emerged—tragic, comic, lyric, exotic, quaint, fantastic?

This chapter has probed many aspects of style and the factors at work in producing it. It should have enabled you to (1) broaden your customary range of moving and responding, (2) find cultural styles that have points of kinship and familiarity with your own style, (3) come to respect and appreciate the ways different historical ideals of what's beautiful, what's good, and what's right have been interpreted and embodied in movement, and (4) use the styles of various art forms to create material for use in dance. The combined effect of all of these will help you realize the validity and integrity of diverse styles. But this is only one step, for as Laban says, "The artist has to represent more than typical beauty. He is interested in all the deviations and variations of movement." You need also develop, as an arist, the gumption, willingness, and desire "to represent more than [the] typical."[7]

11 /
Silence, Sound, and Music

Ideally, the sound score for a dance is the sound of the movement—what the dancer-choreographer hears as she creates her dance. What would happen, then, if the choreographer was doubly blessed, having the ability to compose as well as choreograph? Such a "choreoposer" could produce a score perfectly suited to the needs of each particular dance. Unfortunately though, most of us are not so talented; yet we still must bear the responsibility, as choreographers, of choosing the appropriate accompaniment. That is why it is important to educate ourselves about the possible alternatives. Generally this means considering the three major options of silence, sound, and music. A historical backward glance provides a frame of reference for the first of these.

Silence

In Germany during the early 1900s the purest form of modern dance was Concert Dance, often performed in silence. It was sometimes accompanied by extremely simple percussion, for example, a constant tremor on a gong. Other than that, the silence was accepted as a partner. Only an exceptional dance can be effective when performed in this way. It is not a dance without music, but a dance in silence. It is not a dance without rhythms, but a dance where the rhythms are pulsed in only one place, the body.

Without music leading, supporting, clarifying, or camouflaging, the movement by itself must single-handedly crystalize the content, form, and style, In America, two classic examples of this are Doris Humphrey's *Water Study* and Jerome Robbin's *Moves*.

You have been doing dance studies in silence throughout most of this book. It is time to move in silence consciously and see how good movement sings for itself. Although this does not necessarily mean that movement cannot be enhanced by a sound score, doing a dance in silence gives you an idea of how much responsibility the movement itself must carry. (No longer can you use the excuse, "It's so much better with the music.")

All kinds of movement can work in silence: it can be rhythmic or not, full or sparse, comic or serious. In every case, it carries the power as well as the burden which is created by the absence of sound.

Exploratory Work
Next time you're watching dance on TV, turn the sound off and see what you see. Get your own sense of the audio counterpart to the visual dance, its mood, pitch, volume, tempo. Does the piece work in silence? Does turning on the sound enhance it? Is it simpatico or not, as you expected or otherwise?

Short & to the Point: Inner Music
If movement were an instrument, what tune would it make in your inner ear as you moved? With a variety of movements, create many kinds of inner music. Keep the phrases short. Try it out with these or other images.

haze settling on a prickly pear plant
volcano visiting an octapus den
cradle of cotton candy exploding
a hiccup is a swallow that comes back up

Improv: Conductor's Fantasy
ϙ Imagine you are in a full concert hall conducting an orchestra. Use different parts of your body to evoke a variety of sounds. Hear the music as you move. Know which instruments are playing (brass, woodwinds, strings, or percussion); try different groupings. Indicate changes in tempo, volume, meter. Is it melodic or dramatic, a waltz or a march, a Gregorian Chant or Beethoven's Ninth? (Be careful of overusing your arms.)

Choreographic Study: Symphony in Silence
Using the above improv, choreograph a Symphony in Silence. (Caution: do not be mimetic.)

Sometimes a dance is served by having only a few seconds or maybe a short section in silence. Here the element of contrast adds to the power of the silent movement. In *Primitive Mysteries*, choreographed by Martha Graham to a score by Louis Houst, "the silences, during which all the processionals and many of the key dramatic visions are enacted, are tremendously important. The viewer notices them more, too, because the score avoids melodic development and predictability. The silences break in rudely, commandingly."[1]

Sound

Moving and vocalizing seem to go together naturally: shouts and jumps for joy, moans and hair-pulls in anguish, yells and stamps in anger. Folk dancing often includes singing or shouts of affirmation by the dancer. Why is this so little used in theater dance? Often it's a matter of lung capacity—the dancer and her song are divided and while she dances, someone else sings. They should function aesthetically as one, however, and whether the song is realized by a human voice, musical instrument, or full orchestra, it will still be felt as the song of the dancer.

Verbalizing/Vocalizing

But let's go back to the possibility of the dancer singing her own song. The song may be words—important words used to accent, augment; it may be melodic or disjointed thoughts; it may be the pleasure of playing with musical sounds, the silliness of nonsense words, the fascination of a previously unheard or inner language, or the actual sounds of the human body in motion. Sounds can be as varied and manipulated as movement.

In any of the ensuing exercises you need not verbalize all the time you are moving. Experiment with interspersing voice and moving, having them alternate or overlap.

> *Short & to the Point: Story Dance*
> Spontaneously make up and tell a story, talking and dancing it simultaneously. Some starting possibilities: "The day bubbles and tickles floated in the air . . ." or "The professor announced the scientific effects of taking a bath in globs and glue . . ." or any other you come up with, comic or serious.

> *Short & to the Point: Human Sounds*
> Make and move to giggles, moans, gasps, whimpers, ahhhs, sighs, hisses, snorts, groans, yelps, etc.

> *Short & to the Point: Gibberish*
> Nonsense, no sense, no cents, slow cents, nonsense!! Use nonsense words as verbs to describe your actions as you are dancing them, e.g., "I gardunk when I slorsh, and breem and breem!"

Such verbalizations carry significance and suggest the existence of an inner world that has no known words to describe it. It is a world of raw emotions, fantasy, hidden fears, and ecstasies. It has conventions, truths, structures, and beings alien to what is commonly found in the real world. It is the world of "Jabberwocky."

Choreographic Study: Vocal Sound Study
Using one or several of the above possibilities combining vocal
sounds and movement, create a short study.

Poetry

Often a dancer uses words that do make sense, poetry being
a favorite, and haiku, a special one. Poetry can serve inspira-
tionally as a starting point, providing an image or plot; or it
can be performed as an actual sound score by a dancer or
other figure either in lay or modulated speech or a tape distortion. When poetry is thus used, it should be given the same
consideration as music or any other sound score. Remember,
it is still incumbent on the dance to provide the insight and
carry the message.

The Sounds of Movement

Sometimes the dancer's physical movement provides the accompaniment (inadvertently, as when landing out of a jump,
or purposefully, as with the stamping of feet, clapping of
hands, or floor-skimming swish of a rond de jambe). In tap
and flamenco, the rhythms that the dancer produces are an
integral part of the dance, even a focal point. Here, in truth,
the dancer is her own musical instrument.

Improv: Trapped
◊ Imagine you are on an alien planet, trapped in a large, win-
dowless enclosure. You know your only hope of getting out is
to be saved by one of the strange but friendly creatures there.
These beings have a very narrow range of hearing, both in terms
of the intensity and the types of sound that they can hear, but
once they know you're inside, they'll be able to respond to you
and rescue you. Unfortunately, you're mute and so cannot call
out or make any vocal sounds. Using your body, clothing, or
any of the surroundings, try making all kinds of different
sounds in hopes of finding the one that is of the right pitch,
intensity, duration, quality, so one of the creatures will be able
to hear you. Work for interesting visual counterparts to the

various sounds. Remember, their range of hearing is very limited. Good luck!

Choreographic Study: Soundance

Choreograph a piece in which you consciously employ the sounds made by the body in motion as the sound score.

Nonhuman and Environment Sounds

Nonhuman and environmental sounds (melting snow, railway station, birds) can also be used. Be discreet about what you use and how you use it. Remember what is tedious in great amounts can be effective when hinted at or used carefully.

Choreographic Study: Sound Collage

Make a short tape using primarily environmental sounds. Instrumental sounds (but not music already composed) may be used for added texture. Choreograph to it.

Music

It was a calculated decision to leave music as the last of the three accompaniments considered in this chapter and as one of the later areas to be dealt with in the art of choreography. Many dancers think that choreography is simply a matter of putting movement to music, which makes music the starting point. This incorrectly puts the onus on music to be the initiating agent whereas movement itself is the true core of dance. Nevertheless, while dance should never be subservient to music, music can have tremendous power in determining images and resultant movement for the dancer. The following improv will amply illustrate this.

Improv: Create a World

[There are three variations on this improv, all of which should be done successively.]

⚥ There is an Indian myth: Shiva is asleep on the waters. As he awakens, he creates the world. You are Shiva. As you move, your movements create a world.

First, do it in silence. Then, using these same instructions, do it to Debussey's "La Mer." Thirdly, do it to Ravi Shankar's "Improvisations" or another piece of Eastern music. Allow five to seven minutes for each creation.

Discuss the type of worlds created and how the music influenced the images and resulting movement.

The Dance/Music Relationship

The relationship of dance to music is an intimate one. Music, through its pulse and rhythm, provides a driving force and an overall structure. Its influence can be either positive or negative; the world of dance abounds with the positive successes, and the garbage pail of the dance studio is brimming with the failures. The ideal relationship is when dance and music appear as one, mutually supportive, enhancing one another.

Movement is the source of dance, and music is a related art that is used to help achieve the choreographic intent. When the finished piece reaches performance there should be a synthesis of the two, and music becomes, as Edward Villela says, "the floor that the dancer dances upon."

Now there are times when the dance comes from music, when the music is the direct source for the movement. This is how Balanchine works. He believes that the movement is the result of how the choreographer sees or feels the music and that one of the pleasures for the dancer and the viewer is the relationship between the two. Thus he feels the crucial essence of his work is the intermeshing of the two media to form one statement. Next time you see a Balanchine work, pay particular attention to how he achieves this synthesis. This approach in no way makes the dance a step-child of the music, but rather a sister of it.

Although music cannot make a dance, a poor choice of music can break a dance. A successful piece has good dance, good music, and a good working relationship between the two.

That relationship can originate in one of several ways:

1. ·dance and music composed simultaneously with the choreographer and composer working together;

2. dance created first, with music composed specifically for it;

3. composed music with dance choreographed to it;

4. dance and music created independently and performed simultaneously in a framework of coincidental coexistence, as in the works of Cage and Cunningham (dance and music are not performed together until performance);

5. a working sketch of the dance (including specific movement) is created independently, and then suitable composed music is found (in this, parts of the dance must usually be shaped to accommodate the musical structure, time frame, overall form, climax, meter, etc.).

If you are fortunate enough to have a composer available, do work with him. Before things really get started, brainstorm together and then agree on some basic things such as images, intent, instruments to be used, approximate length. Remember that things often change as the dance takes on a life of its own.

There are no set rules or procedures for working with a composer. The choreographer-composer relationship is as individual as the two people involved. Who takes the initiative? Who adjusts? When it is really working, no one does, because the dance and music, working as and toward a gestalt, together dictate their own progress. Form, content, details—all become self-evident as the dance-music is realized.

Choreographic Studies: Choreographer with Composer
The following are to be done with a composer. If possible, do not dance in your own piece.

1. Choreograph three independent phrases, each one very different from the other. Show the composer. If he plays an

instrument, have him improvise to the phrases. Have him say what he would do musically to your movement. Then discuss your reaction to what he suggests and add your ideas and images for both the movement and possible music.

2. With your composer, mutually choose something to base a study on. Keep referring back to each other, showing or playing themes, clarifying new directions and images. Keep the study short.

3. With your composer, agree on certain parameters for a dance: (a) exact length, (b) general style, (c) form. Then independently choreograph and compose the dance and music. Perform it without any rehearsal or adjustments.

Discuss with the composer which method worked the best for the two of you. What are the things you learned? Any new ideas you would like to try next time?

The nature of the relationship between dance and music can take different forms.

1. It is a one-to-one relationship, like a duet, where both dance and music are of equal importance. (Music visualization, where the score is directly translated into movement, is perhaps the most obvious, though not very profound, example of this. Each instrument has a corresponding dancer whose movement constitutes an imitation of that instrument's music—when the melody goes up the scale, she rises higher in space. In rhythm, dynamics, and phrasing, the dance parallels the music as much as possible.)

2. Music is background and dance is the main focus.

3. Dance is background and music is the main focus (as in opera and some musical theater).

4. Variations in the nature of the relationship exist within one piece, with sometimes the dance and sometimes the music being dominant.

5. It is a conscientiously designed, unexpected relationship between the two, usually resulting in satire, tension, or absurdity.

Music supports movement and acts as a drive mechanism,

adding to the forward motion of the entire piece; it can actually "create a space" in which the dance will live. It can color, underline, tease, converse, and play with the dance. It can be neighbor, friend, partner, lover, enemy. It all depends on the the particular piece of music and how the choreographer chooses to use it.

Improv/Choreographic Study: Your Choice
The five approaches to the origin and nature of a dance-music relationship provide material for improvisations and choreographic studies which are self-evident. Your own needs and interests will determine how many of these approaches you specifically want to work on. A minimum of two studies should be attempted, one which particularly appeals to you, and a second which focuses on an area which is troublesome for you or in which you are weak.

Choosing and Using Music

Regardless of the origin or nature of the dance-music relationship, you'll need to keep these things in mind when working with the music:

Balance. Try to retain a balance between the number of dancers in your piece and the number of instruments playing the musical score. A full symphony orchestra will usually dwarf a solo. Likewise, a group of sixteen dancers will probably demand a fuller sound than a solo recorder. Also, consider the depth or thickness of the sound—a piece played by fifteen musicians could be sparse, whereas (at times) a three-man combo can be full and overpowering.

Style: Ethnic, Historical. Let the flavor of your music match the flavor of your dance. Classical Spanish guitar creates a certain air, perhaps a flamenco atmosphere—use it, don't ignore it. (Even if you ignore the style of music, you must know what it is you are ignoring, why and how you are working against it.) Why choose a Scottish ballad unless you're going to capitalize on that folk form in your dance? If you choose Renaissance or medieval music, know something about the period that it evolved in. This can have implications ranging from the obvious to the sublime—costuming, prevailing social conventions, body movements (gestural vs. postural), and so on. Learn a little about the composer. Get to know about his work and his approach to composition as well as the style he worked in (Romantic, Impressionistic, Neo-Classical, whatever). All of this will contribute to producing a closer kinship between the music and the dance.

Old Favorites and the Top Ten. As tempting as they are, they present problems. For instance, in using vocal music, people often end up either miming the words or having no relationship to them whatsoever. Using well-known pieces, whether classics "(Claire de Lune," "The Blue Danube"), Broadway musical hits, or movie theme songs can be difficult just because they're so familiar; people may already have their own notions, images, and connections (and therefore expectations) of what they're about and can't watch your piece with a fresh eye, ready to see, untainted, what it is that you want to communicate. So, unless it's a conscious attempt at satire, unusual juxtaposition, or period playfulness (John Sousa marches for a patriotic dance medley), these musical memories can harm rather than help your piece. Paul Taylor's *Book of Beasts* is a wonderful example of working with well-known classical music with original and unexpected choreographic rendering.

Be wary of approaching a music composition like the first draft of a manuscript. Not only is it unartistic to delete and rearrange sections arbitrarily; it's often illegal. It would be equivalent to a musician deciding to accompany his four-minute composition with 240 seconds' worth of dance selected in bits and pieces from your seventeen-minute masterpiece—ARGHH!

Another caution here: while it's great to find something that's obscure, make sure it's still available. We remember too well the traumas of choreographing to a favored piece of music only to realize that the present recording is badly scratched, it is no longer available on disc, and so there is no way to get a clean cut of it for the performance master tape. Best bet is to buy two copies, or make a quality tape of your music *before* you start playing it over and over as you work on the choreography. Ideally, if it is published, you could get the score and try to get an ensemble to perform it live.

Of course all of these—balance, style, and old favorites and the Top Ten—have their exceptions. They are meant as guides, not commandments. Learn some music terminology so you can talk knowledgeably with your musician or the composer.[2] In addition, a good music survey course (ideally including classic, folk, jazz, Eastern) will familiarize you with a variety of possible sources.

> *Choreographic Study: Choosing and Using Music*
> Based on the above discussion on choosing and using music, build a short study which primarily deals with the specific considerations of balance, style, or old favorites and the Top Ten.

If you decided on a piece of composed music for your dance, a number of things should happen.[3] First of all, listen to it a zillion times. Improvise freely to it. Get a feeling for the whole and play with any little nuances or themes that intrigue you. Perhaps jot down some short notes (verbal or pictorial) on any special finds. Determine the overall form (compositional structure) of the piece, the meter and tempo for each section and identify the smaller units of phrasing and how they're grouped. As you improvise and develop the dance, keep working back and forth with the music, since it is your partner. Remember when using composed music, it should structure and influence but not dictate the dance.

One way of analyzing your music is to follow the written score and mark out counts, sections, and so on. But let's face it, most dancers don't read music, or even if they do, aren't confortable using that as the device for creating their music outline of the piece that they'll work from in choreography. However, a clearly defined score of some sort really is necessary. For example:

Section I: 12 measures of 3/4, extremely fast
Section II: 16 measures of 3/4, slow
Section III: 8 measures of 4/4, medium fast

Dancer's Counts

The term *dancer's counts* refers to an often used method in which the count patterns are determined by the organization of the movement. The dancer may choose to give every quarter note one count, dividing that count to parallel the movement (fig. 5, version I), or to give each measure one count, counting only the downbeats (version II). (Both of these attend solely to the aspect of timing; dynamic or other qualifiers would be layered over this.)

Rhythm of the Music:	♩	♩	♩		♩	♩♩♩♩	♩	♩	♩	♩
Music's Counts:	1	2	3		4	1234	1	2	3	4

Rhythm of the Movement:	♫	♫	♬	♩	♩♩♩♩	♩	♫	♫	♩
Dancer's Counts, Version I:	1-&	2-&	3-ee-&-a	4	1234	1	2-&	3-&	4

Dancer's Counts, Version II:	1		2	3

Figure 5

Short & to the Point
Try moving to both of the above versions with a drumbeat providing a steady 4/4 pulse.

Sometimes movement counts or phrases are juxtaposed against those of the music such that they do not coincide (or do so only at widely spaced intervals). This is another instance of dancer's counts. The movement rather than the music is the predominant structuring force, and the counts grow organically according to the needs of the movement phrasing.

In such cases it is helpful for the choreographer to write a score that clearly indicates both the music and the dance phrasing and the relationship between them:

Music: six measures of 3/4   (totaling 18 counts)

Dance: three phrases, 5–5–8   (totaling 18 counts)

which, when graphically illustrated, looks like this:

Music   3 3 3 3 3 3

Dance: 5   5   8

Doris Humphrey created the "Variations and Conclusions" section from *New Dance* along these lines, juxtaposing movement phrases of 7–7–10 against six measures of 4/4. It is challenging to the performer and rewarding to the audience as the two independently phrased mediums find their points of union.

Choreographic Study: Dancer's Counts

Create three dance phrases consisting of 5–5–8 counts. Perform this while someone (or the rest of the group) claps six measures of 3/4, steadily counted and accented (six measures of **1** 2 3).

Pick a favorite hit tune or piece of country or jazz music. Determine the meter and number of measures in each verse (eight or sixteen measures are the groupings most commonly used to form a melodic unit). Choreograph several irregular phrases that will total the number of counts in each verse. Do at least four verses. Make sure your irregular phrases are not the same each time (e.g., if each verse had twenty-four beats, you could have 8–3–3–10, 5–4–5–4–6, 10–7–7, 2–8–4–10). Write out your phrases. Perform with music. The stronger the phrasing of your music, the greater the challenge and interest.

Betty Walberg worked out the "Western Woman" section of *Haiku* with this approach. She uses hoe-down music having a regular, recurrent 4/4 rhythmic pattern. She choreographed irregular dance phrases that coincide every thirty-two and forty-eight beats with the music:

Verse 1:	9	9	10	6	6	8			= 48 counts
Verse 2:	5	5	5	5	7	5			= 32 counts
Verse 3:	12	12	7	7	7	3			= 48 counts
Verse 4:	6	6	6	6	7	1		= 32 counts, plus 3 chords
Verse 5:	8	3	5	7	3	9	13		= 48 counts
Verse 6:	5	3	5	3	8	8			= 32 counts

As one gets into modern music (Berg, Ives, Schönberg) it becomes harder to count and follow that score. Dancer's counts become more and more important as the complexity of the music grows. At this point, the dancers' ability to internalize tempo really becomes necessary.

Exploratory Work: Score-a-Score
Choose a short but complete piece of music (this is so you can work with its overall form or compositional structure). It should be fairly simple; Mozart or Joplin are good choices. Create your own score (any self-developed visual representation) to organize and make sense of it. As the framework of your score begins to clarify, label the general sequences, using word-images that capture the essence of the choreographic material, e.g.: 1st section—the approach, formal acknowledgment, gestural, stilted symmetrical movement; 2nd section—an unexpected external event (prop, wind, or torrent), strong and dynamic, fast; 3rd section—intimacy, quiet, postural, with a sustained fading out.

Repeat this process for a complex score.

Live Music

Ideally, live music goes with live dance; so let's try, whenever possible, to be ideal, to use live music. Of course, there's electronic music that is created for (and can only be played on) sound systems: it is taped, spliced, overlayed, and pre-recorded. And there are other sound sources you may want to use that you'd have real difficulty in getting played live (*Songs of the Humpback Whale* or wind and the breaking surf). But for excitement to performer and audience alike, you can't beat live music. As soon as you start working on your dance and know what music you'll be using, get a copy of the score and try to locate musicians who'd be interested in performing it. Then get them to make a cassette recording for you to use in rehearsal so your dancers will be familiar with *their* rendition of the work. Periodically, have a rehearsal with the musicians as the piece progresses.

Improvising with live musicians is yet a further treat for both the dancers and the musicians, but only when both are adept at improvising within their own medium. Musical improvisation, like dance improvisation, is an art unto itself, having little to do with technical ability. Jazz groups are especially good for this, or students from a music composition class. If neither is available, then dancers can accompany for each other with rhythm instruments.

Improv: My Dancer/My Sound

This calls for an equal number of dancers and musicians, with each musician having a different instrument. The musicians decide amongst themselves, prior to the improv, which dancer each one of them is going to accompany (without letting the dancers know). It is each musician's independent responsibility to match, to parallel as closely as possible, his sound to his dancer's movements. The dancers begin, work through, and complete an improvisation as a group. (They may wish to set in advance some framework or theme for their dance improv.) In this improvisation, the dance is leader; the music, follower. When the improv is over each dancer tries to identify which musician was playing her sound score.

Then, of course, there's the turn-about of this, the musicians freely improvise and the dancers select one instrument that they're going to follow. In this case, the music is leader and the dancer, follower. At the end, the musicians have to identify who their dancer was.

Improv: Musical Corners

The musicians distribute themselves around the edges and corners of the studio. They may clump themselves together in small groups of two or three, or be alone. The dancers begin in the middle of the floor. There's an emphasis placed on traveling in this improv—for as the dancers begin to move around the room and approach (or orient themselves) toward a particular musician (or ensemble), that musician begins to play in response to, and in harmony with, the dancer's movements. While the dancer is in the vicinity of the musician, they play off each other with a sense of give and take, lead and follow—a dialogue. When she takes her leave, he likewise lets the accompanying sound fade out. The dancers circulate around the room, going from one corner or musician to another, staying as long as they wish at any one place.

Note: See the improvs on the reverting canon (p.114) for another live music improvisation.

After you've experienced these, make up instructions for an improv for the next time you work with musicians. Maybe that improv will work so well it will inspire the creation of a new dance.

12 /

Group Work

One of the finest pleasures in life is dancing with others—
with one special person or as a part of a group. Dancing
together has all the satisfactions of dancing alone plus the
excitement, involvement, complexity, and contagious enthusiasm of moving with others. In it, one gives up some part of
one's individual initiative in order to submerge, merge, become part of the group.

Group Trust, Movement, Design

Group improvisation, choreography, and performance necessitate intersensitivity and physical contact. Building the
trust that allows this takes time. Exercises in group sensitivity
provide a warm-up for this period of familiarization. They
develop trust of self in relation to the individuals within the
group and to the group as a whole. By the time most dancers
reach performance ability, they're used to the physical contact
that occurs between dancers. But what we are mainly interested in is consciously developing intersensitivity in a way
that fosters the creativity of the group as a whole. In later
improvs, it is this whole group-as-one-unit sense that can lead
to interesting choreography.

173

Exploratory Work: Trust Circle

In groups of four, five, or six. One person stands in the center with eyes closed while the others form a circle around him. The center person, staying rooted in one spot with feet together, keeping his body straight and inflexible, starts to tilt off-balance in one direction. The members of the circle gently push him back toward center. As he becomes more trusting that the group will catch him, he's allowed to lean further before they recenter him. Everyone takes a turn being the center person. Take a few minutes to talk about it afterward.

Exploratory Work: Coffin Pass

The entire class or large group forms two parallel lines, two to three feet apart, facing each other. One person stands at the end of the "people hallway," his back to them, and starts to lean back (as though lying down). Immediately, the end people take the weight of his head, neck, torso, and begin to pass him (head first) down the hallway, supporting the various parts of his body weight from underneath as he gets passed along. At any given time, three or four pairs of people are supporting his weight. The person being passed should keep his eyes closed, hands relaxed, and remain limp—a passive, dead weight. After a while he is carefully put down and the next end person in line begins his journey in the same manner. Continue till all have had a chance to be passed.

Multibody Movement: Design and Structure

When one body uses or reacts off another, you alter and extend your movement possibilities (for example, pushing off another can allow higher jumps). You emphasize the motional aspects of multiple bodies by using each other's weight and energy and the momentum they produce together. Contact Improvisation employs this basic approach.[1]

Improv: Mutual Motion

With a partner, find movement that comes from one body bouncing off another, dragging or being dragged, spinning each other around, carrying or being carried.

A quieter approach can lead to an emphasis on design-effective results.

Improv: Equipoise
In pairs, face each other, holding each other's wrists, with toes touching. Lean back, pulling out and away from each other. While counterbalancing in this way, explore ways of moving, going to the floor and back up again, lifting or extending one leg. It does not matter if you do not both weigh the same; the balance is achieved by the equipoise attained between you as each person constantly pulls away from her partner.

Choreographic Study: Two Is Better Than One
As a pair, jointly choreograph a study that capitalizes on the active and passive movement possibilities of two bodies.

Multiple bodies allow movements and designs simply not possible any other way. There is also the possibility of using two or more bodies as one, creating what amounts to an optical illusion. Murray Louis has a wonderful three-headed worm dance; *The Nutcracker Suite* has the giant mother with a bevy of children finally issuing out from under her skirts; Nikolais repeatedly uses multiple body forms to produce his images. But Pilobolus is the group that has probably focused and capitalized most on the possibilities for producing single creatures by using multiple bodies.

Improv: Shiva
Line up three to six people one behind the other, the front person facing a mirror. Experiment with the visual effect (to an audience) of one figure having multiple arms (as the god, Shiva), as well as the emergence of extra heads, torsos, legs from behind the single frontal figure. Explore ways of changing till everyone has had a chance to be first in line—but let the change occur within the framework of the Shiva image (you can't get out of the line and go around the group to change your position in the line).

Improv: Chair

Two people create different kinds of chairs (with their bodies) for a third to sit, lie, rock on or be carried in.

Choreographic Study: Multibody Creature

In groups of three or four, experiment with ways of being one creature. Become attached in different ways. [You may want to do it with one person sitting out and giving feedback and instructions.] Keep an awareness of the whole creature. Some parts of one of the bodies can be hidden (so you end up with, for instance, two legs, two torsos, three heads); use surprises, play with optical illusions. Set a short study.

There is also the approach of using bodies as structures or design, either as interesting background or as actual apparatus (sets) for other dancers to move on.

Improv: Body Building

[This can be done in small groups, with only one mover, or in larger groups with many dancers acting as the structure and several others simltaneously exploring the mover role.] Build a simple structure with bodies, (a jungle gym, a wall). Make sure it is strong and can support external weight and tensions. The mover or movers then get to play on this structure, moving in, through, with it. As they do so, the structure people have the option of making single simple movements and then refreezing to adjust in some way to the mover(s).

Partner Work

We are social beings, seeking contact, intimacy and communication, receiving friendship, learning, and help. We get into confrontations of all kinds. Now and again we find that special one-to-one relationship where "I" meets "thou."

The relationship of partners, coupled with the physical potential of two bodies working together, is a special concern for the choreographer. The essence of a true duet is that each performer is essential to the whole. It must be done by two and only two. It is not a solo done by two bodies that could just as easily be repeated on four or more. If one person is not there, the dance just won't work.

Improv: The Conversation
Stand or sit facing each other. Be aware of self, of your partner facing you, of the two of you as a unit. You will have a movement conversation with your partner. Move when you have something to say. Your partner will respond in movement and you will answer accordingly. Touch, gesture, and facial expression may all be contributing elements. There is no reason why you can't both be moving at the same time, but remember to listen and not just talk; it *is* a conversation. ♀ Begin . . .

Short & to the Point: Three Duets
1. Time: "Fast is your opinion, slow is mine . . . an argument . . . a resolution."
2. Energy: Same as above using two movement qualities.
3. Space: Same as above using two aspects of space.

Now you're getting to the essence of pair work, an involvement together with a shared focus and objective. This can lead to simple visual designs that are always fun to explore. The various possible shapes created by two or more bodies are an extension of the symmetrical/asymetrical work done in chapter 5.

Choreographic Study: Symmetry and Asymmetry for Two
With a partner in front of a mirror, design three symmetrical positions and three asymmetrical positions for two bodies *acting as a unit*. Incorporate at least one position in constricted space and one in expanded space. Put them in a satisfying sequence with simple direct transitions. Consider that a symmetrical position with two bodies can be obtained by standing behind each other as well as next to each other. Of course in the purest analysis, it is only possible to create a side-by-side symmetrical shape if both bodies are approximately the same size and contour.

Numerical Possibilities and Staging

As the number of dancers grows, so do the possibilities of relationships for dramatic situations and so does the fascination of playing with numbers in a purely classic mathematical sense. For instance, if you have two people there are just two possible combinations: one against one or two together. If you have four people you have five groupings: four individuals; a couple and two individuals; two couples; a threesome and one; or four all together. And this by no means exhausts the combinations possible for a quartet. For instance, in the three against one configuration (fig. 6, no. 4), any member can be the odd man out, the single figure. So within that grouping there are four possible manipulations. All in all, given the permutations of the above five groupings, there are fifteen possible combinations for a quartet.

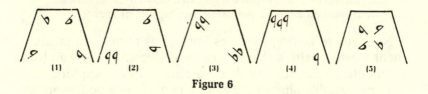

Figure 6

This, by the way, doesn't even take into account that you can also have some of them offstage or holding a position and serving as background. So in a dance of four there can be solos, duets, and trios, as well as the four dancers working as a unit.

Balance and Placement in Overall Design

In becoming competent with the process of choreographing works for larger groups, it's important to use and apply the concepts in this chapter in light of the larger picture, namely, what is happening in the whole dance and how the entire stage appears at any given moment. Sometimes our involvement with specific movements or sections can sidetrack this fuller perspective. Be sure to consider such questions as: (1) What would a time lapse picture of your dance look like? (2) Where are your dancers on the stage? What is their spatial relationship? Is there a concentrated use of one area and if so, how does that serve your choreographic intent? (3) Does the design of one grouping complement the other? (4) Have you maximized the use of various facings? (5) Can that beautiful but delicate movement/design by a solo dancer on stage right hold its own against the group down-left?

Exploratory Work: A Dance for Eight
Chart in detail a dance for eight people using: (1) the whole group as a unit; (2) the whole group on stage flowing in and out of smaller groupings of trios and quartets but with continued attention on what everyone is doing; (3) dancers going on- and offstage leaving various small groups alone onstage. The dance should follow some dramatic or mathematical necessity.

As mentioned in chapter 5 (p. 54), there are choreographers who approach stage placement in a traditional, purposeful manner and those who do not. In Cunningham's dances "no part of the space is more important than another, and each dancer is his own center. This leaves up to the audience the selection, often from a multiplicity of simultaneous activity, of what to look at."[2]

Choreographic Study: Two Stagings
Create several phrases of movement and teach them to a group of dancers. Using only that movement, and keeping other factors constant, create two different studies—one version in which the stage placement is determined in such a way as to emphasize certain movements or dancers (using spatial placement to direct the eye of the audience) and one in which the same movement material is presented democratically, leaving the choice of where to look to each individual spectator.

Discussion. Compare and contrast the results of the two versions.

Small Groups

As you start working in threes, fives or eights you give up more and more of your identity to the larger whole. Each dancer not only has a mutually reciprocal influence but affects the entire gestalt. Once formed, a group works as a unit (though it may be a shifting, flexible unit) until it dissolves or reaches resolution. The members share a motivation or goal and consequently also share a common fate: what happens to the group affects each member.

Just as a duet is not two solos, so a trio is neither three solos nor a duet and a solo. A trio, by definition, is a weaving of three people. Of course, various relationships exist within the weaving, such as two against one, one against one against one. The classical story of the third party breaking up a couple is a prime example (Glen Tetley's *Pierrot Lunaire*).

Improv: Trio—The Eternal Triangle
In groups of three. Two of the dancers working as a duet establish a repetitive movement theme. A third dancer enters and tries to force, tease, seduce one of them away. Let it find its own resolution.

Improv: Quartet—Two against Two
In groups of four. Two people working as a unit establish a movement theme. They keep repeating it while the other pair establish a counter or complementary theme (next to them, going around them, coming at them). Each couple works as a unit and responds to the other couple. Let it find its resolution as a quartet . . . the couple relationships may dissolve.

From now on the choreographic studies may either be choreographed by the dancers in the dance or by an "outside" choreographer. A lot depends on the practical aspects of your situation. You would probably get more out of it if you choreographed by yourself on others, unless, of course, you have to repay your obligations by being in all their dances. It would be best to approach the choreographic studies in this chapter as succinctly and directly as possible. In other words, keep them short and to the point. Also, at this more advanced stage in your choreographic development, use music or a sound score whenever possible.

Exploratory Work: Images for Small Groups
Think of well-known dances that necessarily involved a given number of performers (e.g., Limón's *Moor's Pavanne* as a quartet, Philobolus's *Untitled* requiring six bodies). List dramatic situations and images that imply duet, trio, or quartet. Include both simple and complex images. Some may spur movement ideas (e.g., two people swing a child, a three-legged race) while others can suggest ideas and structure for a whole dance.

Choreographic Study: Trio or Quartet
Using one or more of the images from your list, choreograph a dance using a trio or quartet. Consider the following: (1) numerical possibilities, and (2) staging, balance, and placement in overall design. Give primary consideration to the absolute necessity of three or four participants.

While some classic relationships seem to call for a specific number of people (lovers, mother and child, the eternal love triangle), the number of people used in a dance really depends on the choreographer's vision and main focus. To illustrate this, we will take one classic story (The Garden of Eden) and imagine choreographing two versions of it with a different number of dancers in each.

Version I: a duet in ABC form
A   Eve and Adam are in Paradise enjoying their carefree existence and love.

B   Eve is tempted to look beyond, succumbs, and is expelled with Adam.
C   Together they enter a world of tensions and difficulties.

Version II: A group dance
A   *Paradise.* Eve and Adam are in Paradise enjoying their carefree existence and love (duet).
B   *The Temptation.* The snake tempts Eve (duet).
    The Conscience Speaks. Eve faces the decision alone with her conscience, represented by a group (solo vs. chorus).
    The Decision. Eve and Adam take the apple from the snake (trio).
    The Expulsion. While the snake watches, God expels them from the Garden (quartet, *or* trio with theatrical effects as God).
    The Confrontation. God confronts the Snake (duet *or* solo with theatrical effects as God).
C   *The Aftermath.* Eve and Adam encounter the World Population, tensions, and obstacles as represented by a group of eight dancers (duet vs. a group).
A' *Paradise Revisted.* A memory of Paradise (duet).

See how the form changes from a simple three-part duet to a complex form with internal substructures (A, five sections of B, C, A'), needing four soloists and a group of at least eight other dancers. Here it is evident how form follows content producing organic form. Besides adding people, the priorities of the choreographic vision have changed. No longer is the emphasis on Eve and Adam's love relationship. The temptation and decision (B) goes from a mere transition to a major concern with elaborate detailing of relationships. The innocent love duet (A) goes from being a major half of the work to being an introduction. From a simple duet in the first version, C gains a group and grows in complexity and length in the second version. Because the piece becomes so complex there is a need for a rounding off, a remembrance of what was lost, a return to Paradise—hence A'.

Chorus vs. Group

Also notice in the above example how a number of dancers can be used either as a chorus or as a group. The Conscience (chorus) acts as a multitude of one with a single intention and voice, while the World Population (group) has many facets, divisions, and approaches. In a chorus there are no individuals. A chorus is more apt to have movement in unison (e.g., the circle of twenty or so men in Maurice Béjart's *Bolero* egging on the pulsating female vamp in the center).

Choreographic Study: Chorus and Group
Using five or more people, choreograph a sequence using them as both a chorus and a group, employing some dramatic or mathematical necessity to instigate the change from one use to another.

Exploratory Work: Myth
Find a myth or classic story and write up how you would arrange it for two different size groups.

Discuss how the change of vision accounts for the change in numbers. How do you decide how many people are in a dance? The Garden of Eden example shows us that while the number is not intrinsic in the story, it *is* integral to the choreographer's interpretation.

All this is nice, but often rather idyllic. External, irrelevant, but very practical factors often force the decision of how many dancers to use: there are only three people in your company, you have only one friend who can dance, or there are only four people who are free at the same time you are. Such factors necessitate flexibility in the creative inventiveness of the choreographer.

New Resources: Dances from Your Dancers

A choreographer's main sources are self and the relationship of that self to people, feelings, things, ideas. As you start choreographing on others, a whole new resource opens up to you—each dancer has technical skills plus personality, style, and creativity. As Doris Humphrey says, "this mining for gold . . . is one of the chief rewards of the choreographer, as thrilling as the work of other explorers and adventurers. If [he] does not respond with enthusiasm to such adventure, he possibly does not have the temperament for a life of composing."[3]

The relationship of the choreographer to his dancers is not often discussed except in such mystical terms as a dancer telling how her choreographer "keeps finding new me's that I never knew existed." The specialness of the relationship accounts for the fact that many dancers and choreographers remain together for years, developing, strengthening, and nurturing their creative individuality via their mutual creativity, going deeper and finding ever fresh nuances. Doris Humphrey was one of the first "miners of gold," and a supreme one. Paul Taylor and his company are a good contemporary example of this. Many of his pieces emphasize and are built around the uniqueness of the individuals in his company.

When a choreographer teaches movement to a dancer, he begins a process of molding. The movement is fashioned to that dancer and that dancer to it. If this occurs during the creation of the piece, the dancer influences the creation by how she responds. At the same time, she brings her skill of receptivity (of sensitively interpreting and rendering true the choreographer's intent), allowing herself to be molded.

Often the process goes a step further, as when the choreographer guides the dancer in an improvisation and then uses the new material in the dance (see p. 143). In such cases, the working relationship contributes to the creation of the actual movement material. But no matter how much the choreographer uses his dancers' improvisational movement for material, the ideas for improvisation are still his, the feedback and manipulation during the improv are his, and the choices about whether, where, when, how, and if to use the material are his. It is *his* dance.

Whether or not a choreographer works this way, he still has to consider and fit the movement to particular dancers. Too, he needs to create an atmosphere within which they are willing to give their most subtle and passionate expression. He has to inspire dedication and devotion to the dance and to him.

By this time, you've had a variety of preparatory experiences for working in a group—in a one-to-one relationship, in pair and group improvs, in observing and critiquing others' works, and in choreographing for another student's style. Now you're ready to explore the process of distilling material from the dancers you've chosen to work with, from those who will dance in your piece. This process includes leading them in an improv.

> *Discussion.* What have you noticed about people who have led improvisations you've been involved in? What approaches and attitudes seem to work best? What would you want to remember and try to incorporate when you are the leader? How about these for starters: (1) making it fun, (2) being specific when using images, (3) keeping it simple and movement-oriented, and (4) being responsive to what's happening.

> *Improv: Choreographer-Created*
> Create a structure for an improv from which you hope to glean some material for a dance. Maximize the resources of your dancers, paying attention to their movement styles, body types, and sizes. While the group watches, five dancers take turns leading each other in an improv. Give the improvisers feedback pertinent to the development of your idea: "That's good. Now try it faster. Stay with it and see where it goes. Oh, nice, nice. Repeat that, yes." When necessary you give new directions, stopping and starting again, asking them to repeat or remember a given move or segment. You can also take quick notes or sketches. You can shape some of the material, loosely set it, and have them try it out right then.

The choreographer, dancers, and observers can discuss what happened. Depending on available time, you can proceed to set and try another improv, find new material, throw away extraneous material, and so on.

Choreographic Study: New Resources
Make a short study using the above approach.

A choreographer's dance rides on its performers, so cast carefully. If you have the luxury, pick your people to match your idea. If you don't, capitalize on your restrictions. In effect, this amounts to organic casting. If your resources are limited to your company, your students, your friends, take advantage of the situation and let your people (your living material), with their personal abilities, tendencies, and idiosyncracies, be the seedlings for your dance. People are exciting in their differences—use it! Instead of trying to force someone into a predetermined role, devote that same time, energy, and attention, to finding his unique potential and developing it to your advantage. If you have a beautifully lyric but relatively noncommunicative dancer, *use it.* If you have a supremely dramatic or emotional dancer, but she's technically poor, *use that.* Don't try to find a midpoint, and thus settle for a watered-down version of both. Probably neither you nor she (nor the audience) will be excited about the results. Simply put, make the best of what you've got.

Choreographic Study: Made to Order
Find two or three dancers. If you aren't already familiar with how they move, get to know them through improv, by watching them in class as they perform their own work, or in daily behavior. Find some reason for these people to move together. Choreograph a short piece for them, capitalizing on the uniqueness of their movement styles, affinities, and their physical sizes and shapes.

Using Choreographic Devices and Compositional Structures

Some of the choreographic concepts presented in chapter 8 cry for realization on groups. The following improv and choreographic studies for small groups may either be used as is or elaborated on and overlaid with characters and images. You can learn a lot about manipulation of movement on groups by observing the exercises below, so have some people watching while others are improvising.

Improv: Motif and Development with a Group
Set a motif (see pp. 101–07).

1. Have one person do the motif small; have a group do it large. Try it again with a gradation: one person small, two people a little bigger, three a little bigger, etc.

2. Have one dancer perform the motif as is, then have another do it backward and a third upside down; they can then pass it back and forth like a football.

3. Have different size groups stationed around the stage. Each try the motif in a different rhythm.

4. Same with a quality change.

5. Same with each group doing it on a different body part.

6. Make the entire group travel in one development of the motif, except for one person who travels in a different development of the same motif.

7. Develop the motif in such a way as to make the dancers relate to each other.

Choreographic Study: Motif and Development with a Group
Choreograph a motif and development for a group using the list on pages 102–04 as refresher and motivation.

The above work takes a choreographic device and applies it for use with a group. You could use the same device to create a piece of choreography that is jointly composed by the group working together.

Choreographic Study: Group Choreographed Motif
and Development
One person presents a motif. Everyone does it. Someone creates a manipulation on that motif, shows it, and everyone repeats it. Another person presents another manipulation on the original

motif and teaches it to the group. The original motif, manipulation 1, and manipulation 2 are done in sequence. Continue to have people contribute new manipulations, teach them, and add them on to the sequence. Each contributor has the responsibility of being sensitive to the overall shape that the sequence is taking on (i.e., when it is wanting to build to a climax, when it is leveling out or dying down) so that his addition helps to maintain and achieve an ongoing continuity. This can result in a democratically cooperative choreographic experience.

Choreographic Study: Minimal Movement
with a Group (see p. 110)
Create a study using minimal movement with a group. Consider: Does the entire group speak the same message all together or one at a time? Is there only one tiny voice amidst a grand tumult? Do members of the group take turns with variations on a given minimal movement theme?

Choreographic Study: Canon (see pp. 111–16)
For four or more dancers, create a dance incorporating the canon device.

Compositional structures are likewise enhanced when realized on groups.

Choreographic Study: ABA' with a Group (see p. 94)
Choreograph ABA' for a group. Use different numbers of people in each section.

Choreographic Study: Rondo with a Group (see p. 95)
Create a rondo using various combinations of dancers for the different themes B, C, D. A keeps a constant number and movement theme.

Choreographic Study: Theme and Variation
with a Group (see p. 100)
Set a theme and create different variations using various numbers of dancers for each.

Formations

When working with a large group as a unit, one of the considerations is the formation or overall shape of the group. Ritual and folk forms traditionally use lines (or rows) and circles. Lines can face each other (for courtship and warlike dances), spiral, serpentine, or trace their way through a maze. Circle dances may focus in toward the magic center, out to protect the center from intruders, or move around the rim in a symbolically eternal progression. Both of these forms are fairly symmetrical in and of themselves, but can be choreographically placed off-center and juxtaposed against any other forms or number of dancers to add interest. Other formations include geometric masses (rectangular units, triangular wedges) and amorphous masses.

Improv: Form-a-Line

This improv is done in groups of five or six and will be composed of several parts. In each part you will be asked to group yourselves into a particular formation. Your only restriction is that once formed the group must maintain that formation until the next one is called out. You will have three to five minutes to move and work in each. Although within that time the shape of the formation must remain constant, it may change in size, move around the room, confront or respond to another group. Experiment with the different possibilities for action and interaction that each of the shapes suggest.

Form a line.
Form a circle.
Form a triangle.
Form a square.
Form parallel lines.
Form a bunch.

A variation on this would be to have different groups pick different formations and improvise on them at the same time. Discuss some of the results.

Choreographic Study: Formation
Create a study using various formations of the group for maximum effectiveness. As you are creating the movement that occurs in the formation, keep in mind that one way to give a feeling of unity is to use similar or repeated body designs on several dancers at once.

The One and the Many

The results of group formation make us more aware of the strength in action that groups have. There is power in numbers. The more dancers doing the same movement, the louder it speaks.

Short & to the Point: Power in Numbers
One person assumes an angry stare with stylized stance facing the audience. Others join in same pose, two people, then three, five, eight, twelve, everyone—then one again.
Discussion. How did the exercise change with many dancers as opposed to one? How did you feel as it returned to the original staring figure? What if she then made a radically different movement statement? Suppose the others remained stationary while she danced joyously around them or crept from behind. Sometimes a very powerful statement can be made by a solo figure counterposed against the rest. It adds complexity, gains interest, and highlights or contrasts the power of the group.

Similarly in music a continuous repetition of a given theme serves as background while a single predominant voice rises over that. The theme is referred to as *basso ostinato*. Such a solo voice can present a contrasting or complementary commentary to the theme. In dance, a group could take on the base theme and thus serve as background for the solitary contrapuntal voice.

Improv: Solo and Group (basso ostinato)
Everyone learns a short rhythmic (four measure) phrase, which is fairly stationary and lends itself to repetition. Form a

group in some background part of the stage (across the cyc, up-left in a huddled mass, etc.), and begin doing the patterned phrase in unison. In her own time, one dancer at a time emerges from the group, moving as she wishes to in relationship to them. The group keeps the power of the pattern with clarity, perhaps producing a hypnotic effect. The solo figure has the rest of the stage for herself. She develops a short solo, invested with any power or image she chooses, resolves it, and ultimately returns to take up her part as a member of the group. Another dancer emerges as the next figure, improvises his solo, and returns—and so on, until everyone in the group has had this opportunity.

It should be noted that in the above improv the group performing the basso ostinato functions as a chorus (see p. 183).

Choreographic Study: The One and the Many
Create a study using a group of four to six against a solo figure.

Working with Masses

Exploratory Work
Bring in pictures of mass scenes, throngs, mobs. Include both pleasant and disturbing ones. Share. Identify distinguishing features. What characteristics differentiate a mass, a crowd, a mob, a swarm, a horde?

An interesting phenomenon occurs when more than an identifiable number of people comprise a group. They become a crowd or mass; they act as one; mob mentality takes over. It is primitive, not rational; it is slow in getting started, but once momentum is gained, difficult to stop or change. It can be fascinating to witness, yet when it takes asocial directions, is horrifying and frightening and can lead to destructiveness. Participating in it renders the individual mindless. Such a single-minded mass is a highly dramatic tool, powerful and compelling. It is extremely effective with a large number of dancers, although a strong effect can also be obtained with lesser numbers. The essential thing is that the movement is executed with clarity and precision and performed with a strong drive and focus.

Improv or Choreographic Study: Masses
Structure an improv or choreograph a study for a mass. Take advantage of its monumental proportions.

13 /
Theatrical Elements

Dance as a performing art is bigger than life. It is presentational. As such, the world of theatricality is a part of it, granting access to the use of props, costuming and make-up, lights and sets. At one extreme, this can lead to multimedia productions, using every aspect of theatricality; at the other, it results in minimally staged happenings.

Ideally, theatrical elements are an integral part of the dance. Martha Graham refers to sets as characters, powers on the stage and not decoration. This can also be true of props. Costumes can serve another purpose—to extend the real and illusory design possibilities of the human body in movement (as in Nikolais's *Imago*). All three help define historical or environmental aspects. Sometimes they serve representationally (as in Kurt Joos's *Green Table*) or symbolically and therefore are indispensible. Sometimes they provide special movement possibilities (a place to swing from or climb on; a rope to whip with, tie, or hang from).

Occasionally a prop takes on the characteristics of a set. A "propset" is environmental while being manipulatable. Usually large, it has the dual flexibility of being handled and used by the dancer as well as creating significant changes in the stage design itself. A parachute would be a good example of this. So would a network of anchored and free ropes. Some things can be all three—costume, set, and prop. In

Music for Word Words Steve Paxton deflated a transparent plastic twelve-foot square room around him until it became his costume.

> *Improv/Choreographic Study: All-in-One*
> Find a single article that could be used as costume, prop, and set. Improvise with it in all ways. Choreograph a short piece that capitalizes on its versatility.

When any of these articles are used as a functional part of the dance, it (or an equivalent substitute) must be available for rehearsal. They must exist not only in the choreographer's mind, but be tangibly present in the studio. When theater elements are purely decorative, that is a different matter. In these instances, they are something the designer creates to provide an atmosphere or to embellish the theatrical presentation, thereby adding an extra dimension to the staging of the work.

Facial treatment using masks and make-up can also be functional or decorative. Although sometimes considered the finishing touch, it should not be overlooked in the developmental process of creating and staging a dance. At its simplest, make-up serves to enhance the dancer and improve the audience's discrimination of facial definition and expression. It can be used to draw attention to one particular part of the body (eyes or mouth). Taken to exteme, full body make-up can, in and of itself, wholly define a character (as the gilded idol in Makarova's production of *La Bayadère*). Obviously, the stronger the make-up, the more dramatic its effect.

Masks (whether full or partial) can be used for proclaiming neutrality or establishing identification. The latter function can be achieved representationally (as in commedia dell'arte) or abstractly (Erick Hawkins in "pine tree" from *8 Clear Places*). When used in conjunction with the costuming, masks can produce complete design, as is the case in Oscar Schlemmer's *Triadic Ballet*. Full face masks should always be rehearsed with extensively because of their physiological and sometimes inhibitory effects on movement.

We can and must attend to all these theatrical elements. Yet the viewer's perception will be *primarily* triggered by none of these; the human eye responds to two things, light and motion. That is why we said in chapter 5 that lighting as well as movement can affect which part of the stage is strongest.

Short & to the Point
Close your eyes and visualize two dancers onstage, equidistant from the audience. One is fully lit but still; the other is dimly lit but moving. Which one do you watch?

Any change in lighting causes an automatic physiological response in the viewer. Aside from the purely mechanical ability lighting has to attract our attention, it creates and defines space. Lighting can create boundaries as strong and believable as a brick wall; it can isolate one place from another and ultimately can define that space as warm-friendly, cold-dangerous, or effervescent-ethereal. The larger realm of lighting design sometimes includes or employs other technical effects (film, slides, projections) as well in order to serve specific choreographic needs.

Color (hue and intensity) and form (line, design, and shape) are given primary consideration in working with any theatrical element. Each is a complete discipline unto itself. Every choreographer should have as much exposure to each of these theatrical subject areas as possible. We will touch here only briefly on some basic experiences to initiate an awareness of them.[1]

While theatrical elements may grow out of the needs *of* the dance, they are also of great value as inspiration *for* a dance. They should not be added on simply because they're available or look like fun. For the work presented here you might have to begin by using what is available and then let the ideas for improv and assignment grow out of that. We'll present a range of "beginnings of ideas," but since every prop room or home has its own inventory, see what you have and then let spontaneity reign. Be a scavenger—then take off on images, structures, and ideas that your treasures call forth.

Improv: Props

Simply open your eyes wide and look around. Heavy elastic, dowels, balloons, blankets, ropes, bubble gum, cellophane, mirrors, cardboard cylinders, skateboards, umbrellas, etc. Find what movement is available in or with the props; how they affect what you do and how you do it; experiment with the props in pairs or small groups. Sit down afterward and discuss some ideas that come to mind for choreography with them as crucial parts of the dance.

Improv: Sets

Here again, the sky's the limit. Sure, try a parachute—it's been done before, lots of times, but that makes it no less intriguing. Use chairs, benches, platforms, ladders (three of them, maybe, of different sizes and shapes), and don't always set these in their usual manner; lie one of the ladders on its side, chairs in groupings, some facing forward or back or turned over. Create an environment with boxes (either cardboard or wooden ones to go through, in and out of, around and under). Don't forget the scaffolding.

Improv: Costumes

Getting the idea? Okay. Raid the costume room for long skirts, capes, hats, shoes. Move with them on. Try a modified technique class. How does the costume affect your movement? What characterizations does it suggest? Design an elaborate costume. Structure an improv for it (solo or group).

Exploratory Work/Improv: Make-up and Masks

Take out your make-up and any stage make-up available and try creating many faces (emphasizing different features, blanking out some, abstracting others). What other objects can be added to augment the design (hair-do, feathers as eyelashes, etc.)? Using any full-face mask (even a paper bag with eye holes will do), dance strenuously with it on for three minutes. What physical or emotional effects does it have on you? Design and construct a mask.

Improv: Lights

Try a dark stage except for one spot. Dance with it, around it, in it. Try a duet for flashlight and dancer, done in pairs with a dancer and an offstage flashlight "operator" who flashes the light on, off, around the dancer as she moves and responds to the light. Try a strobe light, finding a clever or dramatic reason to use it.

Choreographic Study: Total Dance

Outline a dance in which the lighting, costumes, props, make-up, masks, and set design are an integral part. Write it out on paper. Have sketches of ideas ready to show the various designers. Choreograph some movement themes in which the particular theatrical element(s) would be involved. Then show your sketches in class, explaining the specifics, e.g., where, when, and how the item will be used and what the requirements will be. Show movement themes with the actual theatrical element (or appropriate substitute). Discuss and get feedback on the integrity and aesthetic value of your ideas and choices.

Remember, your relationship with a good costume, set, or lighting designer is as crucial as the one with your composer. You turn them on with your ideas, requirements, and visions. Then they work on it, adding their own creativity and extended visions, incorporating their expertise and knowledge of what is practical and what is possible. This in turn influences you to mold, spark, or trigger other ideas and solutions relevant to your piece.

The house dims, the lights come up. "Go music. Go, dancers. . . . "

14 /
Performance

The dancer dances the dance . . . they are one . . . there is no separation. Thus the dance lives each time it is performed. Nuances are played with; the shading shifts; the dance deepens, grows. . . .

The choreographer hands the dance over to the dancer, steps back, allowing her to be free within it, and in effect says, "Now it is yours—yours and the audience's—make of it what you will as a performing artist." The choreographer realizes that the magic interaction between performer and audience, the subtle play between dancer and spectator, is an absolutely vital part of the performing art. Can it happen at the end, a sudden and unrelated responsibility that the choreographer lays on her dancers? No. It must be cultivated, nurtured along the way. As choreographer, you develop a trust in your dancers, in their talent and their ability to portray your creation, to bring it to life, to give it existence. After all, you are the one who chose them to be the instrument of your design and utter your message.

There comes a time in rehearsal when the choreographer must resist the temptation to interrupt and give corrections. Let the dancers get the sense of the whole, on stage, in that setting; let them take on the responsibility of its presentation, giving them a chance to respond on the spot to a costume tear, a forgotten cue, a fall; let them work out all these quirks as though it were a live performance.

As it develops, the dance changes, takes on shape, and finally comes into its own, wherein it exists as a separate entity, an artistic expression, a piece of art. Dance and dancer merge. This is a difficult and yet most necessary step. There is no way to effect separation between the dance and the dancer (because a dancer is a medium like paint or a violin); but there is a very necessary separation from the choreographer.

Bit by bit your dance has moved toward that precarious phenomenon that a live performance is. Performance arouses implications and suggestions in the perceiver, making the same dance different for different people. Yes, the input of the spectator is part of the life of dance as a performing art. Movement is full of symbolic meanings, generalized feelings, vague overtones. The choreographer consciously utilizes many, but also employs many more unconsciously, intuitively, and may be surprised to learn of the images it triggered in the audience's eye. All this happens in those never-to-be-repeated moments of the live performance.

What makes an inspired performance? What is the secret that results in those magical moments when the dancer, your dancer, becomes a total instrument, an artistic voice? What is that intangible something that makes an imprint on the perceiver? What is left when all else is taken away, that which the audience has when the curtain has gone down? It is the total involvement of a body and being expressing the symbolic intent of the dance.

> I see a web within a dancer that is taut, lit up when she is "on" and sort of hanging limply when she is not. The web looks like a nerve system. It connects every part of the body with every other part. It connects the hand with the foot even if the focus of the movement at the time is on the hip. It radiates from the eyes, sparks off the spine,

alights between the ankles. Because she is psychically as well as physically aglow, it is no longer a question of a dancer *doing* a dance, but *being* the dance. This web pulses with energy, radiating out, affirming an aura, projecting to the last row of the balcony.

15 /
Tangents

The illusions about the realities of dance soon fade as the realities about the illusions become clear.

The art of dance is spoken *through* not *with* the body.

> ALL IMPORTANT THINGS ARE NOT
> GRAND BIG STATEMENTS:
> TO EMPHASIZE YOU DO NOT NEED TO HIT
> A PERSON ON THE HEAD.

The obvious often goes unseen because it is obvious; but the subtle, the aside, the throw away, catches the attention, lingers, haunts, t^i_ck$_l$^{e}s.

Jumping is to soaring as improvisation is to choreography.

Dance is a prime example of the Taoist principle: "Each thing contains its opposite." For dance is an illusion. Did you ever hold a dance in your hand? Touch it? Smell it? Yet to create this illusion, you need the reality of the articulate human body sweating and thumping along.

The inside me knows how it feels . . .
The outside me knows how it looks . . .
Both me's help me remember and assess it.

The only constant is change.

Dare to be simple.

Movement Plagiarism: This is a concern that crosses all our minds at some point or another as we make our way into the field as a creator, be that as choreographer or teacher. The question arises, "Are movements sacred or are they like words or colors, there to be used by everyone, a common heritage?"

Your dancers are human beings; they are also your clay.

Choreographing is cajoling, seducing, struggling, tampering, pampering, loving.

While the only constant is change, and change is essential, sometimes one changes and changes and changes and comes full circle; sometimes one changes and changes and changes and . . .

The drive for completion is balanced by the pleasure of the process.

Life is about opposites working against each other; from a larger perspective this is essentially the same as working for each other.

How does it feel to climb into your own pocket? How do you know when you are in?

It is better to have a dance too short than too long, to have an audience go away wishing for more instead of wishing for less.

The Impromptu Choreographer: When you find yourself choreographing as you drive on a freeway, walk down a crowded city street, ride in a bus—know you are not alone. At any unpredictable moment, a choreographic idea strikes; you find yourself marking it with your arm, stepping the pattern with your feet, drawing the design in the air. This moving-to-one-self is one of the earmarks of a choreographer, a side effect of the trade, an occupational hazard.

A tao of choreography: If you have nothing worth throwing away, you probably have nothing worth keeping.

While complexity for its own sake may be a fun intellectual or physical game, it rarely survives as art.

Who hasn't known those devastating doldrums when "it just won't come," when you've spent hours in the studio trying to work through a particular transition or brilliant image without producing a moment's worth of useful choreography? There's no way to make it go fast. Time is as inherent in the creative process as it is in growth. When it's not working, don't take on the role of a meatpacker stuffing a sausage. Creating a dance is not the same as jamming your down-filled sleeping bag into its nylon bag. Respect creativity's whimsical nature. Make friends with serendipity. Have faith in yourself and in the creative process.

The performer's challenge: How do you simultaneously create illusion and reality?

Must dance mean?

Be a conductor, not a container, of energy.

Don't put in what you think will impress. It will only appear as something put in in order to impress.

Your dancers are your clay; they are also human beings.

When art is good enough to involve and stimulate the senses, it is senseless to ask, "What sense does it make?"

Allow yourself the creative option of the blunder. Follow the mistakes, the funny tangled paths; investigate the stuck spot; look into the slip-ups, the illogical pests.

Which have you found to work for you . . .
   the more you learn, the more you see things as different
   the more you learn, the more you see things as the same

Some things are too simple for beginners . . . trying to get to the essence of something is advanced work.

Another tao of the choreographic process:
   pare down   build up
   eliminate irrelevancies   add pertinencies
   simplify   elaborate
   focus in   expand out
   with an eye to detail   with an eye to the whole

This I know . . . what I know best, I cannot speak in words.

~~When in doubt, cross out~~.

All along, the choreographic process should have an element of daring and risk-taking; otherwise, nothing new in movement or concept will be created. This should be balanced by a conservatism that doesn't allow novelty for novelty's sake.

The moment of now is forever becoming and that is the moment of dance.

"If anything at all, perfection is finally attained not when there is no longer anything to add, but when there is no longer anything to take away."—Antoine de Saint-Exupéry

Teacher's Addendum / *Appendix* /
Notes / Index

Teacher's Addendum: The Delicate Art of Teaching Choreography

And a delicate art it is—but for all the delicacy there are the practical aspects as well. Besides carefully considering what to teach (content), and how to teach it (method, approach), you need to be sure that the ideas, structures, and themes you use are specifically geared to the point you're trying to get across, that the examples you choose are truly illustrative, and that the experiences you provide are particularly capable of being effective and successful. (If you haven't already done so, read the Preface, Terminology, and chapter 1 which contain some pertinent information regarding the theory and implementation of the material in this book.) Many natural and beneficial things will and do automatically happen when people go through the process of improvisation and choreography; but if there is a consciousness of the process by the teacher, she can facilitate, channel, and encourage it, building a learning experience that is less haphazard, more fruitful, and thus more successful.

The first and most crucial thing to be concerned with when using the "teaching choreography through improvisation" approach is to establish an atmosphere in which the students can trust themselves, you, and each other. This means allowing a certain degree of privacy and anonymity during the improvisational process, without outside observers. It means that you, as leader, are supportive, nonjudgmental, and noncritical in the improvisational part of class; and while continuing to be supportive in the choreographic part, you are honest in using your expertise to give constructive, critical feedback, feedback at *their* level. This will vary from student to student. Some will be ready for critique of a more complex nature, while others will require attention to the most obvious and basic choreographic principles. Try to incorporate this attitude not only into your own comments and suggestions, but help guide it into those of your students, so they will develop a discriminating eye and their comments will be of greater help to each other.

When meeting a class for the first time, it helps to discuss some of the concepts that the class is based on, and the methods that will be used in learning them. Make it clear what you think they should get out of the class. Establish an open rapport. Talk with them about what they think choreography and improvisation are, and about the relationship between the two. Discuss, too, the definition and value of involvement, the fact that you need to be present in order to be involved, the uselessness of the "warm body" syndrome (here in body but not in mind or spirit). Furthermore, make it clear that the creative movement of improvisation, while often imbued with a sense of playfulness, does so within a structured framework that has a purposefulness to it (to be taken seriously), and that playfulness shouldn't be misconstrued as self-indulgent or dismissed with a flippant, offhand attitude of "Oh, we were just playing around." It carries an obligation to the self, the group, and the process.

It is important to encourage your students to approach each choreographic study with the same interest and respect as they would a full dance. With this in mind, the studies are not dead ends; they are wholes unto themselves which may also serve as building blocks or beginnings for more extended work at some future time.

Once the class is underway, another type of discussion enters into the process; these will be about the improvisations and choreography that are happening. Such discussions provide valuable opportunities for the students' expression, reflection, and feedback. They are an integral part of the learning process.[1] It is up to you to encourage those discussions—they become more pertinent and valuable with experience. It is also up to you to guide the discussions in a constructive fashion so that they go beyond the subjective level of "It felt good" or "I like it; it was interesting" and attend to the specifics being dealt with. Coax the students' perceptual responses by guided questioning on the particular concept. (The discussion on page 40 is a good example of this type of directed discussion.) As they improvise more, compose more, and hear other people's comments and ideas, they'll gain a wider perspective and add an objectivity to their own understanding and resultant commentary. Encourage your students to speak to the positive aspects of what they saw and felt as their main observation, "That first part really worked for me. The movement was clean and sharp, like fireworks. But at the end you just seemed to stop. Why not try . . . ?" When they offer such a suggestion of a change, the choreographer can not only say how he feels about the observation, but can experiment right then and there (in a quasi-improvisational way) with making some change, assessing it himself, and getting immediate feedback from the others watching.

The external observer (in this case, one's peers) is both a necessary and tremendously helpful ingredient in the process of learning choreography. But after some experience in dance improvisation, it is time to make the students aware of the additional possibility of staying fully involved while simultaneously observing *themselves* in movement: they can observe what they are doing as they are doing it. Liv Ullman says of her acting, "I experience it at the same time as I am standing outside, watching."[2] Part of the awareness sees the movement from the outside. This observation is essential for remembering, developing, and refining movement for choreography and can add to the depth and enjoyment of the experience itself. It facilitates group work by allowing a view of the total field that adds appreciably to the sensing and perception of that group. In so doing, one can become aware, from the craftsman's point of view, of what is workable choreographically. It is important not to start this too early, so that it does not lead back to self-consciousness; rather it is consciousness of self in movement which is desirable. The capacity to observe oneself is not constantly in operation; that's fine, so long as the first priority remains on the involvement in the movement.

Achieving some sort of balance between the objectivity of observation and the subjectivity of involvement is not easy. The problem is that in improvisation class, everyone moves most of the time, whereas in choreography class, everyone sits and watches, discussing one person's work. Here are some ways to get more watching into improv class and more moving into choreography class.

After the whole class has improvised, let half of them improvise on the same idea or the next step in its development, while the other half watches. They see how their peers actualize the same stimuli. Cite the differences as well as the universalities and the similarities—and encourage both. There can be discussion or not afterward.

One method of providing for some choreographic feedback, without taking the enormous amount of time necessary to show each piece individually, is to have the students pair off and show each other their studies and discuss them. This method allows the student to give as well as receive feedback on a very safe level. It serves as a transition to the sometimes inhibiting situation (especially for the beginner) of showing a study in front of the entire class. It encourages the observer of the pair to be discriminating in what he sees and to verbalize it. The pairing method forces students who might otherwise shrink from verbal participation (which necessitates a consciously focused and articulated evaluative expression) to bring their perceptions to the surface.

In other peoples' studies we find our own problems, tendencies. We find solutions or approaches that we'd perhaps never think of by ourselves. We find camaraderie and support in their struggles and successes. This in turn helps us see our own work with a fresh eye. When the group comes together after showing and discussing in twos, you can ask, "What did you learn from these?" This provides a quick survey and summary. The method of showing in twos provides a chance to see others' work, to perform, and to give and receive constructive criticism quickly and safely.

It cannot be emphasised enough that the learning of choreography consists not only of the creation, preparation, and showing of pieces (and of the need to receive and apply critical, supportive feedback), but also of increasing one's ability to perceive, distinguish, and specifically identify (observe with awareness) the concepts, techniques, process, and craft of choreography as present in the works of others—both on one's own level of learning and more advanced, including the master choreographers. Through films and live concerts that supplement classroom choreography, students should be encouraged to dissect and discuss critically and openly their appraisals and ideas concerning works by professionals. It is not only valid, but ultimately quite useful to deal critically with highly reknowned pieces of choreography; it is another way of identifying which concepts are becoming clear and which are still difficult or misunderstood. Students should be expected to justify their critiques, remembering that there are many right answers, depending on personal aesthetics as well as variations of intention. Being able to look objectively at one's own work is inextricably linked with gaining skill in perception of the choreographic elements in others'. This process of improving perception (and the ability to see, identify, and evaluate) is a skill that improves with practice.

Often in discussing a dance, an improvisation, or a choreographic assignment, one asks whether or not it "worked." It works when there is a feeling of satisfaction, of involvement, of communication, and when (in the instance of choreography) something happens between the performer and audience. This is not necessarily something that can be easily translated into another medium like words. People (performers, improvisers, audiences) often feel that a piece works and have a sense, a simpatico, or merely an "Ahh, yes . . . ," but can't explain why or tell you two words about what it means. Even though you can't explain this phenomenon, you can express it. "It worked!" is great for any choreographer to hear, even if you can't tell them how or why. After more experience in translating your responses into words, you will be able to.

Another and quite separate point to consider is whether the study fulfilled the requirements. In each improvisation and study, the student should try to capture the central concept without embellishment, distraction, or confusion with other themes. This will allow him to explore the central idea to its fullest, with all its subleties and shadings. In the discussion, keep the specific instructions in mind and talk to that point (e.g., stage space, motif and development). If the central concept does not come through clean and strong, identify what other things got in the way. Realize, however, that the "did it work" appraisal and the "fulfilling of the study's focus" question may at times be mutually exclusive. And it is extremely useful for the choreographer to be made aware of this distinction so she can know what it is that she's succeeded at and what she's ignoring, avoiding, or having difficulty with.

The following are some of the questions that could be used in such discussions. Expect, accept, and make it clear that these will have multiple responses.

Did it meet and attend to the central core of the assignment? How?

How did it feel? Can you identify what was happening at the time you felt that?

Was the length determined organically or did it seem arbitrary? What things contributed to producing that effect?

What was the unifying element, the central theme? How

was variety used? Was there too much, making it muddy, scattered?

What was its best moment? Why?

What was the high point (in the case of a phrase)? The climax (in the case of a fuller study or whole dance)? How were they achieved?

If you could make one change or suggestion, what would it be?

Then there's the question of intent: "What did you want to bring or do to your audience?" This is perhaps less suitable for the very short dance study than it is for a larger piece and a complete dance, but it is essential to keep in mind and to challenge the choreographer with, for it is definitely a critical issue. (Intentionality is specifically covered in chapter 2.) Knowing this, watch out for (and teach *them* to watch out for) that self-indulgent tendency of explaining their dance. They must always remember that the movement must speak for itself.

For each improv, present the basic information containing the essential images and the developmental potential. Do not indicate what the resulting movements will be because *there is no right way* for an improv to emerge. This must be a creative experience; no value judgments, please. The improvs are meant to aid in the learning experience of a particular choreographic concept. You only need to keep your dances on the track so that they are participating and therefore learning, exploring, and defining the concept at hand. Other than that, *you should not try to influence the outcome* so that it meets your preconceived ideas. "Choreography cannot be taught," said John Martin, "it must be elicited."[3]

Elaboration of an improv includes allowing for the images that follow from the main one and attending to details. Students and teachers are sometimes concerned with a need to stay with the given image. It pays to point out that an image in an improvisation simply provides a starting place. If the improv does not seem to be working, you have to use other words, a different approach, substitute concrete images for abstract ones (or occasionally, vice versa). Of prime importance is that your instructions be immediately translatable into movement.

Many things come into play in the integration that results in the creation of a dance. The choreographer's whole life, personality, and education form the matrix from which she creates. The teacher's role is to help one little part of that complex matrix become well-defined and integrated, and this is only made possible by providing a context in which what's being done is relevent to the student. The improvisations and choreography will take on the needs of your students and your particular orientation, verbal style, and feeling for imagery. In other words, they will be colored by both your and your students' creativity. It will be *yours*.

When leading, you must tune in to what is happening. You give images and timing to the dancers . . . you take images and timing from the dancers. You are mutually responsive instruments:

The art of leading is following.
The art of teaching is learning.

And you in your teaching will be learning the delicate art of teaching choreography.

Appendix:
List of Improvisations and Choreographic Studies

Improvs and choreographic studies are listed here, by chapter, in the order in which they appear in the text. Choreographic studies are printed in boldface type. An asterisk marks those improvs which are also choreographic studies.

Chapter 3. Speaking Body

Body Discovery
Body Parts
Back-to-Back Conversation
Mirroring

Mirror Corridor
Blind Shaping
Leading

Chapter 4. Phrase

Impulse—Tilt
Breath*

High Point*
Mixing Phrases

Chapter 5. Space

Levels*
Directional Patchwork
Directionality
Dimensionality—Height
Egyptian Frieze

Table Top
Curved or Straight-and-Angular
Computer
Man-on-a-Stick
Symmetry/Asymmetry

Chapter 6. Time

Chapter 7. Energy

Chapter 8. Forming

ABA'
Rondo
Life Cycle*
Natural Progressions
Narrative
Autobiography
Dance Collage
Variations on a Theme
Theme and Variations
Motif and Development
Motif and Development at an
  Advanced Level
To the Glory of Sharmal
Highlighting
Three Punches
Unity-Variety-Contrast
The Smallest Voice

Echo
Reverting—Overlapping Canon
  (visual)
Reverting—Overlapping Canon
  (aural)
Strict Canon
Loose Canon
Canononing
A Chancey Dance for Six (two
  versions)
Picture Score
Score-a-Dance
By Breckenridge Lardé
Two Alternative Ends
Overall Form
Graph-a-Dance

Chapter 9. Abstraction

Mother and Child*
Candle
Abstracting an Image
Wild Kingdom

Gestural Trigger and Response
Gesture Development
Five Degrees of Abstraction
Pure Dance

Chapter 10. Style

Student-Set Improv in Personal
  Movement Style
Self-Style
Atypical Style
For Someone Else
Imitation
**In Imitation of a Great
  Choreographer**
Contraction and Release*

Fall and Recovery
Suspension, Fall, and Recovery
Cultural Style*
Early Man
Primitivism
Supplementary Group Improv in
  Primitivism
Great Periods in Art*
Strangeness*

Chapter 11. Silence, Sound, and Music

Conductor's Fantasy
Symphony in Silence
Vocal Sound Study
Trapped
Soundance
Sound Collage
Create a World

Choreographer with Composer
Your Choice*
Choosing and Using Music
Dancer's Counts
My Dancer/My Sound
Musical Corners

Chapter 12. Group Work

Mutual Motion
Equipoise
Two Is Better Than One
Shiva
Chair
Multibody Creature
Body Building
The Conversation
Symmetry and Asymmetry for
Two
Two Stagings
Trio—The Eternal Triangle
Quartet—Two against Two
Trio or Quartet
Chorus and Group
Choreographer-Created
New Resources

Made to Order
Motif and Development with
Group*
Group Choreographed Motif
and Development
Minimal Movement with a
Group
Canon
ABA' with a Group
Rondo with a Group
Theme and Variation with a
Group
Form-a-Line
Formation
Solo and Group (basso ostinato)
The One and The Many
Masses*

Chapter 13. Theatrical Elements

All-in-One*
Props
Sets
Costumes

Make-up and Masks
Lights
Total Dance

Notes

Chapter 1. Approach

1. Rudolf von Laban (1879–1958) was a German-born movement theorist and choreographer who conceived such systems as Labanotation, Effort/Shape, and Space Harmony. He did extensive work in time-motion studies and founded the idea of movement choirs. His theories, amplified by others, have provided major contributions to the understanding and exploration of movement as a discipline and as an art. See the two books by Cecily Dell, *A Primer for Movement Description Using Effort Shape and Supplementary Concepts* (New York: Dance Notation Bureau, 1970), and *Space Harmony* (New York: Dance Notation Bureau, 1972).

2. Murray Louis, *Inside Dance* (New York: St. Martin's Press, 1980), p. 124.

3. Linda Tarin Chaplin, "Teaching Dance Improvisation Creatively," *Journal of Physical Education and Recreation*, April 1976, p. 42.

Chapter 2. The Essentials

1. Murray Louis, *Inside Dance* (New York: St. Martin's Press, 1980), p. 123.

2. Selma Jeanne Cohen, ed., *The Modern Dance: Seven Statements of Belief* (Middletown, Conn.: Wesleyan University Press, 1966), p. 67.

3. Moira Hodgson, *Quintet: Five American Dance Companies* (New York: Morrow, 1976), p. 13.

4. Louis, *Inside Dance*, p. 161.

5. William Strunk, Jr., and E. B. White, *The Elements of Style* (New York: Macmillan, 1972), p. 72.

6. Cohen, *The Modern Dance*, pp. 35–36.

7. Alma Hawkins, in class at UCLA, 1975.

8. Curt Sachs, in *World History of the Dance* (New York: Norton, 1963), divides cultures into two basic approaches to movement, imageless and image. These are a close equivalent to the above categories.

9. Merce Cunningham, "Choreography and the Dance," in *Dance Anthology*, ed. Cobbett Steinberg (New York: New American Library, 1980), p. 52.

10. Cohen, *The Modern Dance*, p. 24.

11. Strunk, *Elements of Style*, p. 17.

12. Anatole Chujoy and P. W. Manchester, eds., *The Dance Encyclopedia* (New York: Simon & Schuster, 1967), p. 432.

13. Cohen, *The Modern Dance*, p. 24.

14. Ibid., p. 8.

15. Louis, *Inside Dance*, p. 161.

Chapter 3. Speaking Body

1. Curt Sachs, *World History of the Dance* (New York: Norton, 1963). pp. 37–40.

Chapter 4. Phrase

1. Doris Humphrey, *The Art of Making Dances* (New York: Rinehart, 1959), p. 69.

Chapter 5. Space

1. "The High dancer will preferably move toward the higher directions [levels]. His movements in general, will be more tense. This type is the ideal of the ballet, preferred by it and overdeveloped. The Low dancer feels more at home in the lower part of space. His movements will always be stronger and more impulsive than those of the high dancer. The Middle dancer . . . to whom the swing is best fitted, does not incline to either high or low space directions, but moves, in general, on the horizontal. Each individual is more valuable as a dancer in his own characteristic movements, and realization of the different types is of great value in developing them and in staging dances with them." Irma Ott-Betz, "The Work of Rudolf von Laban," *Dance Observer*, December 1938, pp. 4–5.

2. A fuller explanation of these, including more extensive terminology and implications, may be found in Cecily Dell, *Space Harmony* (New York: Dance Notation Bureau, 1972).

3. Alma Hawkins, *Creating Through Dance* (Englewood Cliffs, N.J.: Prentice-Hall, 1964), p. 45.

4. Laban's distinction in Shape Theory between arc and spokelike is applicable here.

Chapter 7. Energy

1. Dr. Valerie Hunt is a noted scholar, analyst, and researcher of movement behavior and corrective physical therapy whose work has ranged from studying primitive people in remote parts of the world to being director of the Movement Behavior Laboratory at the University of California at Los Angeles.

2. Sustained slow high-energy taken to the extreme of stillness produces what is commonly known as isometrics.

Chapter 8. Forming

1. John Martin, The Modern Dance (Brooklyn, N.Y.: Dance Horizons, 1965), p. 35.

2. Silvano Arieti, Creativity: The Magic Synthesis (New York: Basic Books, 1976), p. 377. Italics added.

3. Alma Hawkins, Creating Through Dance (Englewood Cliffs, N.J.: Prentice-Hall, 1964), p. 88.

4. Moira Hodgson, Quintet: Five American Dance Companies (New York: Morrow, 1976), p. 86.

5. Labanotation, although a movement score, is strictly set and involves no use of chance at all. For our purposes, we are referring to scores that are open-ended. See Ann and Lawrence Halprin, RSVP Cycle (New York: G. Baziller, 1970), for a multitude of nontraditional scoring possibilities.

6. Doris Humphrey, The Art of Making Dances (New York: Rinehart, 1959), p. 165.

Chapter 9. Abstraction

1. Ray E. Birdwhistell is one of the foremost authorities in the field of human communication and creator of kinesics, the study of human body motion, and of two transcription systems for recording body movement.

2. John Martin, Introduction to the Dance (Brooklyn, N.Y.: Dance Horizons, 1965), p. 120.

Chapter 10. Style

1. Ben Shahn, The Shape of Content (Cambridge, Mass.: Harvard University Press, 1957), p. 51.

2. Selma Jeanne Cohen, ed., The Modern Dance: Seven Statements of Belief (Middletown, Conn.: Wesleyan University Press, 1966), p. 35.

3. Ibid., p. 81.

4. See Ernestine Stodelle, The Dance Technique of Doris Humphrey and Its Creative Potential (Princeton, N.J.: Princeton Book Co., 1978), pp. 13–18, for a fuller discussion of Humphrey's theory.

5. Moira Hodgson, *Quintet: Five American Dance Companies* (New York: Morrow, 1976), p. 87.

6. Louis Horst and Carroll Russell, *Modern Dance Forms in Relation to the Other Modern Arts* (Brooklyn, N.Y.: Dance Horizons, 1973).

7. Rudolf von Laban, *The Mastery of Movement* (Boston: Plays, Inc., 1971), pp. 88–89.

Chapter 11. Silence, Sound, and Music

1. Marcia B. Siegel, *The Shapes of Change* (Boston: Houghton, Mifflin, 1979), pp. 56–57.

2. The definitive study of music provides analysis of the formal way of ordering time in rhythm, meter, melodic line, note value, etc. Although a basic course (such as Music Education or Music for Dancers) is essential, we see that as groundwork for the material covered here. In no way are we attempting any of this very valuable work. For that, we refer you to Pia Gilbert, *Music for the Modern Dance* (Dubuque, Iowa: W. C. Brown, 1961), especially for its application of music for use by the dancer-choreographer.

3. Be sure to familiarize yourself with current copyright laws covering use of music for performance. Consider if and how they are applicable to your specific circumstances.

Chapter 12. Group Work

1. Contact Improvisation, started by Steve Paxton, is an improvisational form in which two people use and capitalize on the intimate interplay of two bodies' mutual interdependence as the major source for impetus, support, timing, and flow. A shared relationship to a center of gravity is pivotal, as the partners blend their weight in continuously shifting points of contact. It is an inherently improvisational activity. Paxton says, "You can never repeat it on purpose; it just doesn't work that way." Yet, one could choose to use Contact Improv with an eye toward its choreographic possibilities, either including it as an improvised section within a choreographed piece or capturing and giving form to the exquisite moments that do occur during the improvisation.

2. David Vaughan, "Dance of the Avant Garde," in *Dance of the Twentieth Century: Slide Text and Catalogue*, ed. Susan Reiner and Nancy Reynolds (New York: Pictura Dance, 1978), p. 43.

3. Doris Humphrey, *The Art of Making Dances* (New York: Rinehart, 1959), p. 21.

Chapter 13. Theatrical Elements

1. See Joan Schlaich and Betty Dupont, eds., *Dance: The Art of Produc-*

tion (St. Louis, Mo.: C.V. Mosby, 1977), for a succinct and practical book that covers all these areas.

Teacher's Addendum

1. Alma Hawkins, *Creating Through Dance* (Englewood Cliffs, N.J.: Prentice-Hall, 1964), pp. 101–15, covers evaluation thoroughly.
2. Liv Ullman, *Changing* (New York: Knopf, 1977), p. 219.
3. John Martin, in class at UCLA, 1975.

Index

227